The Casework Relationship

The Casework Relationship

FELIX P. BIESTEK, S.J.
School of Social Work, Loyola University

London
UNWIN HYMAN
Boston   Sydney   Wellington

THE CASEWORK RELATIONSHIP
APL230 DISC A1 SIDE 2

Published by the Academic Division of
Unwin Hyman Ltd
15/17 Broadwick Street, London W1V 1FP, UK

Unwin Hyman Inc.,
8 Winchester Place, Winchester, Mass. 01890, USA

Allen & Unwin (Australia) Ltd,
8 Napier Street, North Sydney, NSW 2060, Australia

Allen & Unwin (New Zealand) Ltd in association with the
Port Nicholson Press Ltd,
Compusales Building, 75 Ghuznee Street, Wellington 1, New Zealand

First published in Great Britain in 1961
Thirteenth impression 1990

Printed in Great Britain by
Billing & Sons Limited, Guildford, London and Worcester

CONTENTS

FOREWORD

THE UNIQUE IMPORTANCE of the professional interpersonal relationship between the person seeking help from a social agency
and the caseworker is universally recognized in contemporary
practice. The relationship is the soul of social casework. It is
the principle of life which vivifies the processes of study, diagnosis, and treatment and makes casework a living, warmly human experience. It would be hard to exaggerate the importance
of the relationship in casework, not only because it is essential to
effective casework, but also because it is the practical living out of
our basic convictions about the value and dignity of the human
person. It is based upon a philosophy of life which is both realistic
and idealistic, which encompasses matter and spirit, reason and
faith, time and eternity.

Social workers, ever since the time of Mary Richmond, have
been eloquent about the importance of the casework relationship
but, oddly enough, have been somewhat inarticulate in explaining
what it is. The stress has been laid on the intuitive skills in establishing and maintaining a good relationship; it has been said that
the relationship has to be experienced in order to be understood.
Unfortunately, in some professional circles the impression was
given that the relationship is a pseudomystical experience which
only the initiated could understand.

The reasons for the apparent disinterest in verbalizing about
its nature are easily identified: the pervasiveness of the relationship in the casework process gives it an elusive quality; no explanation or definition can do justice to a living thing; words
have a certain coldness, while relationship has a delightful
warmth. Then, too, social workers are of the belief, and rightly
so, that the skill to establish and maintain a good casework relationship is eminently more important than the ability to define it.

This book is based upon the conviction that there is a real
value for a professional social worker in being able to explain,
define, and analyze the casework relationship. A well-defined
terminology is one of the indispensable conditions for the growth
of a profession. And even though a verbal explanation cannot

adequately convey the full human overtones in a good casework relationship, it can perform a useful function as long as its inadequacy is recognized. Obviously, a conceptual understanding of the relationship does not automatically give skill in establishing and using it; skill can be developed only through repeated, intelligent practice. As in all other human endeavors, however, understanding can be an aid in acquiring skill; knowing the elements of a good relationship may be the first step toward skill.

A good conceptual analysis of the casework relationship can help in the training of students; it will not replace but rather enrich the intuitive approach to casework both in the classroom and in field practice. It should be equally helpful to every caseworker, however experienced, in the self-evaluation of his daily work. Occasionally every practitioner is bothered with the disturbing problem of "What is wrong in my relationship with this client?" It would seem that a knowledge of the elements of a good casework relationship should be helpful in making an accurate diagnosis of that relationship which is "not quite right."

The purpose of this book is to explain, define, and analyze the casework relationship as a whole and in its parts. There are many real dangers in this undertaking. Each relationship in real life has an individuality; in the discussion which follows, the individuality of relationships is somewhat subordinated to the essential, common elements inherent in all casework relationships. Also, the casework relationship is a living, pulsating thing, and living things are injured when dissected. Consequently there is a risk of losing something important in the cutting up of concepts and in studying the elements of a thing whose elements never exist alone.

The author is greatly indebted to his colleagues of the School of Social Work of Loyola University for their assistance and inspiration. He also wishes to express his gratitude to his former students, Mary Scully, Raymond Ganey, and Ann Snelus for their contribution to this study. Special acknowledgment is due to the Family Service Association of America for permission to quote extensively from its publications.

F. P. B.

PART ONE

THE ESSENCE OF THE
CASEWORK RELATIONSHIP

THE ESSENCE OF THE
CASEWORK RELATIONSHIP

SOCIAL CASEWORK has been defined as "an art in which knowledge of the science of human relations and skill in relationship are used to mobilize capacities in the individual and resources in the community appropriate for better adjustment between the client and all or any part of his total environment."[1] The purpose of casework, according to this definition, is to help the client make a "better adjustment"; casework helps a person meet a problem, fill a need, receive a service. The means to this purpose are the mobilization of dormant capacities in the individual, or the mobilization of appropriate community resources, or both, depending upon the needs of each client.

"A knowledge of the science of human relations" is necessary because the caseworker deals intimately with people. In order to understand the individual it is very helpful to know as much as possible about the common characteristics of human nature. The knowledge of how human personality grows, changes, reacts to life's stresses, normally and abnormally, serves as a framework in which the individual client is better understood.

The relationship between the caseworker and the client is the medium through which the knowledge of human nature and of the individual is used; knowledge alone, without skill in relationship, is inadequate. The relationship is also the channel of the entire casework process; through it flow the mobilization of the capacities of the individual and the mobilization of community resources; through it also flow the skills in interviewing, study, diagnosis, and treatment.

The casework relationship is only one species of interpersonal relationships; there are natural relationships such as husband-wife, parent-child; professional relationships such as physician-patient; and many others such as friend-friend, customer-salesman. As in casework, life's interpersonal relationships have a unique importance: they are the principal, possibly the exclusive, source of real happiness.

The relationship between a man and a woman, the central theme of songs, novels, and dramas throughout the ages, is one of the basic sources of human happiness. The difference between a home and a house is not landscaping nor interior decorating; a home and all the happiness it connotes is a situation in which the interpersonal relationships between husband and wife, between parents and children, are good, rich, and satisfying. The ancient adage says that the richest man in the world is the man with the largest number of real friends. Modern industry has learned that the relationships between employer and employee, management and union, employee and employee, are more important for efficiency and productivity than merely good wages. Even the beatific vision is a face-to-face interpersonal relationship between man and God.

Real happiness, therefore, is not found in the possession or the use of things. A certain number of things are necessary for human living, for the satisfaction of common human needs; food, clothing, and shelter are indispensable for subsistence. Things give comfort, pleasure, and satisfaction, but in themselves they do not give happiness. They can contribute to happiness indirectly, but only when they promote satisfying interpersonal relationships. If the father of the family does not provide sufficiently for his wife and children, the interpersonal relationships may suffer. But they do not do so necessarily and automatically, especially if the insufficiency is due to no fault of the father. Not every poor family is unhappy; nor is every rich family happy.

The contrary is equally true: poor interpersonal relationships are the principal, possibly the only, source of real unhappiness. The damage done to a personality through poor parent-child relationships is apparent in child-guidance clinics. Most schools of psychiatry identify poor interpersonal relationships as the basic cause of neuroses and many forms of psychoses. The real cause of every divorce is the breakdown of the husband-wife relationship, as the experience of marriage counselors proves.

The many possible interpersonal relationships have generic similarities, but each has its specific features. The following questions can help to differentiate relationships.

What is the purpose of the relationship? The purpose will largely determine its nature and qualities. For instance, the purposes of the parent-child and the caseworker-client relationships immediately suggest many differences.

Are both parties on terms of equality, and are the benefits resulting from the relationship mutual? They usually are in a friend-friend relationship but not in the teacher-pupil nor in the leader-follower relationship.

Is there an emotional component in the relationship? It is present in the parent-child relationship but absent in the ticket-agent-traveler relationship.

Is it a professional relationship, such as physician-patient, or nonprofessional, as between friend-friend?

What is the normal duration of the relationship? The teacher-pupil is temporary; friend-friend may be temporary or permanent; the parent-child relationship is lifelong.

The casework relationship differs from others on a number of points. It differs from the parent-child relationship in that the casework relationship is temporary, and the emotional component is not so deep and penetrating. The equality and mutuality in a friend-friend relationship is absent in casework. The caseworker and the client are fundamentally equal as human beings; but in the casework situation the caseworker is the helping person, while the client is the person receiving help. Essentially the relationship between teacher and student is on an intellectual level; if an emotional component enters into the relationship, it does so *per accidens* and not as a necessary element for achieving the purpose of the relationship. In the physician-patient relationship the patient at times can be the passive recipient of the physician's services; the skills and the medicines of the physician do the curing, although in most instances the cooperation of the patient is vital. In casework the client does more than merely cooperate; he is helped to help himself. In a warden-prisoner relationship the former has authority over the latter; caseworkers, with some exceptions in the protective and corrective services, ordinarily do not have legal authority. The psychiatrist-patient relationship has the greatest similarity to the casework relationship. The principal difference is in the greater depth of the emotional component in the therapeutic relationship. The psychiatrist's services are directed very frequently to the unconscious life of the patient, while the casework services are directed to environmental changes and to personality problems on the conscious level. In the actual practice of psychiatric agencies, however, the roles of the social worker and the psychiatrist frequently overlap. As a result it is extremely difficult to differentiate the nature of their relationship.

The term "relationship" is of rather recent origin in social casework, dating from Miss Virginia Robinson's book, *A Changing Psychology in Social Case Work*, published in 1930. Historically, social work in the United States started with only a purpose and a motive, and gradually developed a body of knowledge, a technique, and finally a theory. Practice, in every instance, preceded its terminology. Skilled social workers were engaged in the phenomenon which today we call the casework relationship long before they gave a name to that phenomenon. And it took many years before one name won favor over the others.

The earliest term was "friendship." It suggested the humane quality which American social workers sought in helping the poor; it characterized the revolt against the spirit of the Elizabethan poor laws. The vagueness of the term was soon felt, however, and the early strivings toward recognition of social work as a profession spurred the search for a more "scientific" and a more accurate word.

"Contact" was also used, but it lost favor because it seemed to suggest something static. It implied a "touch," principally the metaphorical touching of the client by the caseworker. The real thing, however, was recognized as a two-way process, dynamic and continuing.

"Sympathy" was another of the early terms; it emphasized the emotional component in successful communication with clients.

> Friendly visiting means intimate and continuous knowledge of and sympathy with a . . . family's joys, sorrows, opinions, feelings and the entire outlook upon life. The visitor that has this is unlikely to blunder either about relief or any detail; without it, he is almost certain, in any charitable relations with members of the family, to blunder seriously.[2]

"Empathy" replaced "sympathy" in the terminology of some social workers because it seemed to express a more realistic sharing in the feelings of the client. Professor E. W. Burgess, in his discussion of Clifford Shaw's technique in dealing with problem boys, states his preference for "empathy":

> The first step in the course of treatment is the approach to the boy, not by sympathy, but by empathy. Through his life-history his counselor is enabled to see his life as the boy conceived it rather than as an adult might imagine it. Empathy means entering into the experience of another person by the human and democratic method of sharing experiences. In this and other ways rapport is established. Sympathy is the attempt through imagination to put one's self in another person's place with all the fallacies which are almost necessarily involved.[3]

"Rapport," a term borrowed from psychology, was quite popular with social workers for a long time.

> In effecting rapport, the case worker will be in all interviews warm, natural, outgoing, at ease; she will take definite steps to establish a case work object relationship with the client as the so-called emotional bridge over which factual data regarding the client and his problem will pass to the case worker and back over which interpretations, enlightenment, and guidance will pass from case worker to client.[4]

"Transfer," introduced into social work literature by Jessie Taft, was described as "an emotional relationship to the client."[5] Miss Robinson objected to the word "transfer," saying that it

> is too directly borrowed from psychiatric terminology and leaves the case worker again with a dependence upon another profession and a confused sense of likeness at this point instead of forcing her to analyze her own process in its unique difference from every other professional venture.[6]

"Transference" began to be used by some social workers as synonymous with "relationship," but objections to the word were soon heard.

The term *transference* has become common property in all fields of psychology and connected areas, to the extent that it has become diluted and abused. Psychiatrists and social workers use the term for any kind of relationship, particularly that of clients and patients to worker and therapist. *Transference* should be used only where the repetitional character of the relationship either has been proved or is suspected, although we will have to admit that there is hardly any important emotional relationship in which a considerable amount of transference from earlier objects does not participate.

Of more significance than the name given to it is the description and definition of the casework relationship. Prior to 1940 the literature of social work manifested very little interest in defining it. Even after 1940 the attempts to analyze it conceptually and to define it were no longer than a few paragraphs.

The following excerpts, arranged chronologically, illustrate the attempts to express the nature of the relationship. Very few of the writers formally intended a definition: some merely pointed to a quality of the relationship which they considered especially important; others offered a broad description without intending it to be exhaustive.

1929 The flesh and blood [in social casework] is in the dynamic relationship between social case worker and the client, child or foster parent; the interplay of personalities through which the individual is assisted to desire and achieve the fullest possible development of his personality.[8]

1930 . . . a treatment relationship whose essential characteristic is dynamic interaction between client and worker.[9]

. . . the treatment relationship itself becomes the constructive new environment in which he [the client] is given an opportunity to strive for a better solution.[10]

1935 In the process of both diagnosis and treatment the interview is in reality an interplay of dynamic personalities which constantly act and react to each other's questions and answers, to each other's gestures, facial expressions, manners, and even dress. Generically an interview is a mutual view . . . of each other's thoughts, feelings, and actions.[11]

Whether this process is designated as friendliness, *rapport*, identification, transfer, relation, sympathetic insight, or empathy, it aims to establish a bridge across which an interviewer and interviewee can convey a sense of their mental and emotional natures to each other, whereby they can become "we" in another form, winning across the void which separates man from man and gaining a feeling of kinship.[12]

1940   At all times the case worker must offer a relationship free from prejudice and anxiety, an open table cleared for coöperative action in solving a certain problem. . . . In the chemistry of the relationship between the case worker and the seeker of help, the resulting product depends upon the interaction of ingredients from both parties.[13]

1941   It is the dynamic interaction which takes place between personalities, or better, between personality trends or drives. . . . What happens depends upon the two individuals who, it should be remembered, are participating simultaneously in other relationships. In addition, much depends upon the situation in which people get together.[14]

Relationship, in other words, is the *means* for carrying out function. It must not be looked upon as an end in itself, but instead must remain incidental to function.[15]

1948   The relationship is the medium through which the client is enabled to state his problem and through which attention can be focused on reality problems, which may be as full of conflict as emotional problems.[16]

1949   In its simplest form a *relationship* may be defined as a connection between two persons for common satisfactions or purposes. A *casework relationship* is the professional meeting of two persons for the purpose of assisting one of them, the client, to make a better, a more acceptable adjustment to a personal problem. Within its limits is found the emotional exchange that makes treatment possible. The relationship is the sum total of all that happens between the participants—all the words exchanged, the feelings, attitudes, actions, and thoughts expressed; everything, in fact, that the client and worker do whether open and overt or devious and hidden.[17]

1951 Within the democratic frame of reference the professional relationship involves a mutual process of shared responsibilities, recognition of the other's rights, acceptance of difference, with the goal, not of isolation, but of socialized attitudes and behavior stimulating growth through interaction.[18]

Analogies are abundant in the above excerpts. The casework relationship has been compared to an atmosphere, to flesh and blood, to a bridge, and to an open table. The essence of the relationship has been called an interplay, a mutual emotional exchange, an attitude, a dynamic interaction, a medium, a connection between two persons, a professional meeting, and a mutual process. The concept "interaction" seems to be the most generic, and it was most commonly described as "dynamic."

The material of this dynamic interaction was variously described as personalities; thoughts, feelings, and actions; ingredients from both parties; and the sum total of all that happens between the participants. This all-inclusiveness of the matter of the dynamic interaction raises the problem of distinguishing the relationship from the casework process as a whole; it does not distinguish, for example, between relationship and study, diagnosis and treatment; it seems to presume that the relationship is the total, the synonym for the entire casework process.

The purpose of the relationship was described as creating an atmosphere, the development of personality, a better solution of the client's problem, the means for carrying out function, stating and focusing reality and emotional problems, and helping the client make a more acceptable adjustment to a personal problem. The relationship has general and specific purposes. Moreover, in some cases the relationship is the principal form of treatment, while in others it is an aid to treatment.

On the basis of the description and the definitions of the casework relationship that we have discussed, the following definition has been formulated:

The casework relationship is the dynamic interaction of attitudes and emotions between the caseworker and the client, with the purpose of helping the client achieve a better adjustment between himself and his environment.

This definition will be discussed by considering (1) the purpose of the relationship, (2) the attitudes and emotions that are the material of the interaction, (3) the dynamic nature of the interaction, and (4) the qualities of the relationship.

THE PURPOSE OF THE RELATIONSHIP

In general, the purpose of the relationship is a part of the over-all purpose of the entire casework process: to help the client with his psychosocial needs and problems. In addition, the relationship has more proximate purposes, all of which can be categorized as creating an atmosphere in which the client feels free to engage effectively in the study, diagnosis, and treatment. Since each casework situation is individual, occurring in agencies with different functions and with clients who differ in personality, needs, and problems, the relationship may serve one or more proximate purposes in each case.

For example, one of the proximate purposes in a public assistance agency may be to help the client maintain his sense of personal dignity and human worth as he participates in the details of establishing his eligibility. In casework with an unmarried mother the relationship may serve to dissipate the clouds of emotion which surround the status of unmarried motherhood, thus preparing her for constructive planning for herself and her child; it may contribute somewhat toward the easing of her anxieties; and it can be the beginning of building strength and of renewing energy for her to face a difficult future. In casework with foster children and parents, with children and adults in child-guidance clinics, with parolees, the purpose may be to arouse and stimulate the client to mobilize his dormant capacities or to support him psychologically over a difficult period of his life. In complex cases the relationship may serve many of these purposes.

ATTITUDES AND EMOTIONS

The material of the relationship is an interaction of the attitudes and emotions of the caseworker and client. By "attitude" is meant "a tendency or firm resolve [of the will] to act in a given way under a given set of circumstances."[19] An attitude is a volitional direction based upon an intellectual conviction and in some instances colored with an emotion. By "emotion" is meant a "conscious state of excitement, brought about by the recognition of a stimulating situation, and accompanied by disturbed conditions of the whole bodily mechanism."[20] What attitudes and emotions constitute the material of the casework relationship?

The conviction of the social work profession, distilled from years of experience with many clients in many settings, is that every request for help from a social agency is psychosocial. That is, even in those instances where the client requests a concrete service or a material form of assistance, it can be presumed that some kind of uncomfortable feeling, even though not verbalized or overtly manifested in behavior, is present in the applicant. An emotional component, in other words, inevitably accompanies social needs and problems. This springs, at least in part, from the sense of dependency which applying at a social agency represents. Environmental problems can produce a variety of immobilizing emotional reactions.

The kind and degree of emotion will differ from client to client. The social problem and the meaning of the problem to the client will differ; the ability of clients to cope with life situations, their emotional maturity, their personality strengths and weaknesses, will be different. But within these differences there is a pattern of basic emotions and attitudes that are common, in varying degrees of intensity, to all people who need help, however temporarily, from others.

The sources of these basic emotions and attitudes are seven basic human needs of people with psychosocial problems:

1. The need to be dealt with as an individual rather than as a case, a type, or a category.

2. The need to express their feelings, both negative and positive. The feelings may be of fear, insecurity, resentment, hatred, injustice, and so on, or of their opposites.

3. The need to be accepted as a person of worth, a person with innate dignity, regardless of the person's dependency, weaknesses, faults, or failures.

4. The need for a sympathetic understanding of and response to the feelings expressed.

5. The need to be neither judged nor condemned for the difficulty in which the client finds himself.

6. The need to make one's own choices and decisions concerning one's own life. The client does not want to be pushed around, "bossed," or told what to do. He wants to be helped, not commanded.

7. The need to keep confidential information about oneself as secret as possible. The client does not want his neighbors and the world at large to know about his problems. He does not want to exchange his reputation for the help he will receive from the social agency.

The client may or may not have a conscious awareness of these needs, and he may never formally verbalize them. These needs cause emotions in the client which are somehow manifested in his behavior. These manifestations, observable by a sensitive caseworker, may take innumerable possible forms; they will vary from client to client, and within the same client at different times during the life of the case.

These emotions in the client, in turn, elicit a response of attitudes and emotions in the caseworker toward the client, thus beginning the dynamic interaction.

DYNAMIC INTERACTION OF EMOTIONS AND ATTITUDES

An interaction, in general, is a back-and-forth movement of some form of energy between two or more sources of energy. A conversation is a verbal interaction between two people; boxing is a physical interaction; teaching is an intellectual interaction. In each instance the nature of the energy distinguishes one kind of interaction from another. In the casework relationship the interaction consists of the back-and-forth movement of the attitudes and feelings between the client and the worker.

A dynamic interaction is one in which the movement may change direction or rate of speed, in accord with the purpose to be attained, but which never ceases completely. "Dynamic," the contrary of "static," also suggests a vigor and an inherent necessity for activity. Similarly, the dynamic interaction of feelings and attitudes between the caseworker and the client may speed up or slow down, even within one interview, and its external manifestation may change; but it does not cease as long as the relationship continues. The interaction has at least three directions.

The first direction is from the client to the caseworker. The seven basic needs enumerated above create feelings in the client which are directed toward the caseworker. The client, now in a position in which he must reveal to the caseworker his problem and some of his weaknesses, has a fear and an uncertainty which might be paraphrased as follows: "Will this caseworker listen to my story and treat me with warmth and sensitivity; will he regard me as a·person of worth and dignity, or will he deal with me impersonally as 'a case,' judging me as a failure, forcing me to do something I do not want to do, and divulging my secrets to others?"

The second direction is from the caseworker to the client. The caseworker, sensitive to the basic needs and feelings of the client, understanding their meaning, and appropriately responding to them, wordlessly through his attitude says to the client: "Knowing your problem, your strengths and weaknesses, I continue to respect you as a person. I have no interest in judging you innocent or guilty; I want to help you make your own choices and decisions." Through his attitude, which has some emotional content, the caseworker thus responds to the client and desires the client to see that response.

This response of the caseworker is principally internal. It may not, perhaps, ever be put into words. If the caseworker really has that attitude and feels that way internally, the client will sense it, at least intuitively. If the caseworker does not really have that attitude, the client will equally sense the lack of it, regardless of the verbal protestations of the caseworker. That attitudinal response, moreover, is not established once, at a given point of time, and then taken for granted. Rather, it is an ongoing, continuous, living thing that grows and deepens throughout the casework process. Sensitive diagnostic thinking helps the caseworker recognize the occasions when it is best to verbalize this attitude.

The third direction is again from the client to the caseworker. The client becomes aware of the caseworker's response and somehow manifests this awareness to the caseworker. The client tells the caseworker, wordlessly as a rule, principally through his entire attitude to the caseworker, that he knows the caseworker welcomes his expression of feelings; that he knows the caseworker senses and understands his anxieties and fears, and is accepting and nonjudgmental. If these feelings and attitudes are ever verbalized, they may take the form of simple expressions such as: "I have never felt so free in talking to anyone like this before," or "I feel very good inside after talking with you."

These dynamic interactions, separable only conceptually, are living, vibrant forces that endure in some degree throughout the period of person-to-person contact, and in some cases may continue in residual form even after the case is technically closed as is sometimes evident when a case is reopened.

SEVEN PRINCIPLES IN RELATIONSHIP

To understand a thing well it is necessary to understand its elements. Thus far the relationship as a whole has been discussed. How can the relationship be divided conceptually? The following table illustrates two possible methods of division: the three "directions" of the interaction and the seven "principles."

First Direction: *The* NEED *of the client*	*Second Direction:* *The* RESPONSE *of the caseworker*	*Third Direction:* *The* AWARENESS *of the client*	*The name of the* PRINCIPLE
1 To be treated as an individual			1 Individualization
2 To express feelings	The caseworker	The client	2 Purposeful expression of feelings
3 To get sympathetic response to problems	is *sensitive* to, *understands,*	is somehow *aware* of	3 Controlled emotional involvement
4 To be recognized as a person of worth	and appropriately *responds*	the caseworker's sensitivity,	4 Acceptance
5 Not to be judged	to	understanding,	5 Nonjudgmental attitude
6 To make his own choices and decisions	these needs.	and response.	6 Client self-determination
7 To keep secrets about self			7 Confidentiality

It would seem that the directions are divisions of the interaction, while the seven principles are the elements of the casework relationship as a whole. Each principle necessarily involves the three directions.

They are principles of action, based upon a fundamental truth, which influence, guide, and direct. Depending upon the point of reference, they may also be called qualities or elements: qualities in the sense that they are necessarily present in every good relationship; elements in the sense that conceptually they are the constitutive parts of the relationship.

Each of these seven principles will be discussed in a separate chapter. They are not separable in reality, for each necessarily implies the others. A defect in any one of them indicates a defect in the entire relationship; the absence of any one of them signifies the absence of a good relationship.

It should be noted that in each principle both the caseworker and the client are involved. A number of other casework concepts, intimately allied to the principles, involve only the worker principally or the client principally. Some refer to the caseworker alone. A few examples are self-awareness, objectivity, and the professional attitude. They are, of course, directed toward the client, but in themselves they do not imply the same kind of interaction as the principles do. They are requisite qualities in the caseworker, necessary for establishing a relationship. Some terms refer to the client alone; for example, security in revealing himself to the worker, ability and strength to look at himself objectively, confidence in the caseworker, strength to do what is necessary for constructive change, and so on. This group of concepts can be considered as desirable effects of a good relationship upon the client.

The relationship has been called the soul of casework, while the processes of study, diagnosis, and treatment have been called the body. This analogy indicates a conceptual distinction and a real unity. Both are a species of human interaction. In both there is a back-and-forth movement of some form of human energy. In the relationship the interaction is primarily *internal,* and the energy consists of feelings and attitudes. In study, diagnosis, and treatment the interaction is primarily *external,* and the energy consists principally of words and actions. The unity of these inter-actions in actual casework is similar to the unity of living things. The external interactions may produce, manifest, and affect the internal interactions; the latter, in turn, may affect the former. They are inseparable in reality; without a good relationship the processes of interviewing, study, diagnosis, and treatment are lifeless services.

This is one principal difference between social work and some of the other professions. In surgery, dentistry, and law, for ex-ample, a good interpersonal relationship is desirable for the *per-fection* of the service, but it is not necessary for the *essence* of the service. The surgeon may not have a good bedside manner; the dentist may be inconsiderate of the patient's feelings; the lawyer may be cold and overly businesslike. But if the surgeon operates successfully, if the dentist heals the ailing tooth, and if the lawyer wins the case, they have performed the essential service requested. Not so the caseworker. A good relationship is necessary not only for the perfection, but also for the essence, of the casework service in every setting.

ENDNOTES FOR PART I

1 Swithun Bowers, O.M.I., "The Nature and Definition of Social Casework: Part III." *Journal of Social Casework* 30:417, December 1949.
2 Mary E. Richmond, *Friendly Visiting among the Poor*, p. 180. New York: The Macmillan Company, 1899.
3 Clifford R. Shaw, *The Jack-Roller*, pp. 194-95. Chicago: The University of Chicago Press, 1930.
4 LeRoy M. A. Maeder, "Diagnostic Criteria—The Concept of Normal and Abnormal." *The Family* 22:171, October 1941.
5 Jessie Taft, "The Use of the Transfer within the Limits of the Office Inter-view." *The Family* 5:143, October 1924.
6 Virginia P. Robinson, *A Changing Psychology in Social Case Work*, p. 114. Chapel Hill: The University of North Carolina Press, 1930.
7 Richard Sterba, "On Transference"; in Richard Sterba, Benjamin H. Lyndon, and Anna Katz, *Transference in Casework*, p. 3. New York: Family Service Association of America, 1948.
8 *Social Case Work: Generic and Specific*, A Report of the Milford Confer-ence, pp. 29-30. New York: American Association of Social Workers, 1929.
9 Robinson, *A Changing Psychology in Social Case Work*, p. 150.

10 *Ibid.*, p. 136.
11 Pauline V. Young, *Interviewing in Social Work*, p. 2. New York: McGraw-Hill Book Company, 1935.
12 *Ibid.*, p. 353.
13 Carlisle and Carol Shafer, *Life, Liberty, and the Pursuit of Bread*, p. 180. New York: Columbia University Press, 1940.
14 Herbert H. Aptekar, *Basic Concepts in Social Case Work*, pp. 48-49. Chapel Hill: The University of North Carolina Press, 1941.
15 *Ibid.*, p. 58.
16 Lucille Nickel Austin, "Trends in Differential Treatment in Social Casework." *Journal of Social Casework* 29:205, June 1948.
17 Benjamin H. Lyndon, "Development and Use"; in Richard Sterba, Benjamin H. Lyndon, and Anna Katz, *Transference in Casework*, p. 16. New York: Family Service Association of America, 1948.
18 Gordon Hamilton, *Theory and Practice of Social Case Work*, second edition revised, p. 27. New York: Columbia University Press, 1951.
19 Vincent V. Herr, S.J., *How We Influence One Another*, p. 161. Milwaukee: Bruce Publishing Company, 1945.
20 *Ibid.*, p. 106.

PART TWO

THE PRINCIPLES OF THE
CASEWORK RELATIONSHIP

Principle 1

INDIVIDUALIZATION

THROUGHOUT the centuries the works of charity have emphasized services given by an individual to an individual. Christ pledged His followers to a love of neighbor; that He expected them to individualize their love is signified in the mandate that they love one another as He loved them and that they do to others as they would do to Him. The medieval saint Francis of Assisi, who had what may be described as casework intuition in a high degree, saw through external appearance what a man really was and used psychological means to help liberate the human soul. Later, such practical spiritual leaders as St. Vincent de Paul in the sixteenth and seventeenth centuries and Frederic Ozanam in the nineteenth saw each man, not only as a social being, but also as an individual. Religiously motivated, they directed their aid to the needs of

23

both body and soul of their neighbor, whom they considered a brother in God. They "searched for a man's inner attributes which his obvious failings obscured."[1]

Following the disunion of Christendom and the suppression of church-sponsored charitable organizations came the "dark ages" of public relief, pervaded by the spirit of the iron-hearted Elizabethan poor laws. Unhappily, this inhuman attitude to the poor, with very slow changes for the better over the years, dominated the relief programs in the English-speaking countries for more than two centuries. Throughout this period the individualization of the poor was practically unknown. Its rediscovery took a long time.

The sign of this struggle appeared in the first recorded history of social work in the United States, when the National Conference of Charities and Corrections began in 1880. The delegates to that conference were torn between two major interests: the old, whose concern was for the suppression and control of pauperism; and the new, whose interest was in a more humane individualizing of the poor person. It was the reappearance of the age-old problem, in human garb, of the one and the many.[2]

At the national conference in 1886 George B. Buzelle said: "Classifications of our fellow men are apt to prove unsatisfactory under the tests of experience and acquaintance with the individual. The poor and those in trouble worse than poverty have not in common any type of physical, intellectual, or moral development which would warrant an attempt to group them as a class." Miss Virginia Robinson, in 1930, referred to this statement as the "enunciation of the principle of individualization, the foundation of modern case work."[3]

With the development of the charity organization movement in the United States, individualization of the client began in a rudimentary way, through legal-like "investigation." The emphasis was upon fact gathering, a very cold process. The common methods of helping were advice, persuasion, and exhortation. It took the tremendous influence of Mary Richmond to add warmth to the fact-finding diagnostic process and to reconcile the struggle of opposing tendencies between the welfare of the individual and of society. The process of crystallizing the principle of individualization from an intuitive regard for man to a professional attitude, consciously adopted and systematically developed, was necessarily a gradual process. Miss Richmond gives the reason: "In the early stages of a democracy, doing the same thing for everybody seems to be the best that administrative skill is equal to, but later we learn to do different things for and with different people with social betterment clearly in view."[4]

The essential convictions about individualization, as it is understood today, are contained in the following statement:

> **Individualization is the recognition and understanding
> of each client's unique qualities and the differential use
> of principles and methods in assisting each toward a
> better adjustment. Individualization is based upon the
> right of human beings to be individuals and to be treated
> not just as a human being but as this human being
> with his personal differences.**

Modern casework is client-focused. It relies upon the individual presentation of the problem. Diagnoses are made and goals are planned, individual case by individual case. Treatment is on an individual basis, through the person-to-person relationship. Each client is an individual, each problem is a specific one, and the social service must be based on the peculiar circumstances surrounding a particular situation. This does not mean an adherence to the philosophy of existentialism, which overemphasizes individuality to the exclusion of commonality. In social work the common attributes of human nature and the importance of understanding the common patterns of human behavior are recognized. Social work emphasizes individuality, but balances this emphasis with an awareness that human nature has some basic common characteristics and patterns.

INDIVIDUALIZATION AS A RIGHT AND A NEED OF THE CLIENT

Individualization is one of the essential notes in the concept of "person." Boethius defined person as "an individual substance of rational nature."[5] Human nature itself is common to all mankind, but it is individuated in each person. Each person is individualized by his heredity, his environment, his innate intellectual capacity, his volitional activity, and his cooperation with the grace of God. Each person has different life experiences and different external and internal stimuli. His emotions and memories influence his thinking, feelings, and behavior in an individual manner. Each person's nature is "capable of integrating and directing its own forces in a way that is different from that of every other individual nature."[6]

Since the client is different from others, the help he needs is also in some way different. Casework help, therefore, must be differentiated to meet the particular needs of the individual client and to help the client use his own abilities and resources to work out his problems.

Each person is conscious of being unique. This awareness is especially poignant when he applies at a social agency for help; at that time he has an acute need of being dealt with as an individual rather than as a case, a type, or a category. Even if the caseworker cannot individualize eligibility requirements, he can differentiate the manner of helping the client establish his eligibility.

The client comes to the agency in a state of heightened sensitivity. The client needs the worker's "undivided attention, privacy, and help in discussing the topic of greatest interest to him— namely, his situation and request."[7] The client will recognize the caseworker's attitude if he "is encouraged to tell his own story and describe and give his view of his situation. He feels understood because of the worker's respect for him as an individual with rights and needs, but particularly because of the acceptance of his feeling about himself, about coming for help, and about his immediate situation."[8]

The client's awareness of the individualization by the caseworker will produce desirable effects, principally a constructive use of the agency. If the caseworker has reviewed the available data prior to the interview, the patient is "likely to respond favorably to the social worker's inquiry as to whether what he knows of the patient's situation corresponds with the patient's view of it."[9] If, however, the client feels a lack of attention, he "reacts by giving the bare objective facts of his case rather than his subjective feelings which are often the most important items."[10]

Only as the client feels recognized as a particular individual and feels understood with his problems will he be able to enter into a helping relationship. The success of the relationship, therefore, rests on the individualization of each client.

THE ROLE OF THE CASEWORKER

The skill to individualize professional services is the result of appropriate attitudes, knowledge, and abilities. A number of prerequisites in the caseworker can be enumerated:

1. *Freedom from bias and prejudice.* Since the removal or the softening of the causative factors in the client's problem is frequently the goal of treatment plans, a correct identification of the causal factors and a certain degree of objectivity are necessary. Biases and prejudices can impel a worker to impose preconceived cause-and-effect patterns upon clients in the diagnostic process. These biases can pertain to people belonging to certain races, to people applying for financial assistance, to unmarried mothers, to natural parents seeking temporary foster-home care for their children, to relatives of patients in mental hospitals, and to many other kinds of persons requesting service.

An honest and frank self-awareness of the caseworker's personal feelings, needs, and countertransference tendencies are necessary. "The truth is that there are mixed motives in the best and worst of us; so one of the essentials in treating others is understanding and facing ourselves."[11]

> All the things said about understanding human beings apply also to the interviewer, for he too is a human being, with unconscious as well as conscious motivation, ambivalence, prejudices, and objective and subjective reasons for his behavior. He brings to his relationship with the interviewee his own predetermined attitudes, which may profoundly affect that relationship. He has a natural tendency to impute to others his own feelings and may thus seriously misunderstand his client's situation and problem.[12]

2. *Knowledge of human behavior.* A knowledge of the patterns of human behavior is necessary, however, as a framework within which the individual is understood and helped. It guides the caseworker in securing the significant facts and in discovering the true situation. A caseworker's own life experiences are helpful but inadequate for effectively understanding the various people who come to social agencies. "Common sense" is a tremendous asset, but in the professional day-to-day service to people it needs to be supplemented by knowledge and insight derived from the sciences, principally from medicine, psychology, psychiatry, sociology, and philosophy.

3. *Ability to listen and to observe.* Hearing and seeing are the principal avenues of learning the individual. The client needs to talk, and the caseworker needs to listen. The more the client is enabled to tell his story in his own way, to tell of his own feelings, the more the caseworker learns. The worker gradually comes to see the person as he moves about in his family and community relationships. He sees the wholeness of the social situation, together with the individual's feelings and problems relating to this whole.

The client wants and needs someone to listen to him, not just in a friendly way, but in a competent, professional way. This means that the worker is expected, not merely to listen, but also to hear. The most vital concerns of the client may not be expressed loudly, explicitly, and formally, but rather softly, hesitatingly, and possibly hidden subtly. Only careful listening to what the client is saying, and to what he is not saying, can result in hearing the pertinent material.

Seeing the unverbalized expressions of emotion in the face, the eyes, the hands, and the posture and in the speech hesitations and phrasing can help the caseworker understand the individuality of the client. The client cannot say everything he would like to say about himself, but he can reveal much, perhaps unknowingly and painlessly, through his manner.

4. *Ability to move at the client's pace.* As the caseworker sees each client, he must be able to begin where the client is and to proceed at the client's pace. This is a detail in individualization which can help the client participate fully in the study, diagnosis, and treatment process; insensitivity to the client's pace can stall the entire helping process because the client feels that the caseworker is "taking over." Correct pacing is the secret to the timing of every stage of the casework process, from the appointment for the intake interview to the terminating interview; it guides the fact gathering, the analysis and interpretation, the determination of the treatment goals, and the use of resources. Pacing is the guide and the test of individualization.

5. *Ability to enter into the feelings of people.* The feelings of the client are his most individual characteristics. Problems produce different feelings in different individuals. Individualization, then, requires a sensitivity and a response to these feelings. The principal quality of the response is warmth. "To be useful to another who is trying to change himself and his attitude, the social worker must have a gift for intimacy. He must be willing to enter into the feeling experience of the client, willing to listen to his view

of his problem and of his experience, willing to go patiently along with him in his struggles for a solution."[13]

6. *Ability to keep perspective.* The emotional involvement, however, should be controlled and directed to the total situation, so that the caseworker constantly maintains a perspective. This perspective helps him to see the feelings as they are related to the objective situation and the individual as he is related to his family and social situation.

> We were apt to forget the client in his entirety. In our desire to meet his feeling needs, we overlooked his physical ones. In our haste to understand his unconscious motivations, we sometimes forgot his conscious desires. We became blind to the interplay of social, physical, intellectual, conscious, and unconscious emotional factors in our haste to learn and practice the latest technic.[14]

MEANS OF INDIVIDUALIZING

Although the internal conviction of the caseworker that individualization is vital to effective helping and the real desire to live this principle in practice is paramount, individualization can and should be externalized, so that the client cannot fail to feel it. The following list of suggestions is only illustrative, but it contains a few practical means for individualizing and for transmitting the individualization to the client.

1. *Thoughtfulness in details.* Thoughtfulness in details, such as making appointments, is an indication of individualization. If the client is a mother of several small children and is asked if an appointment hour would conflict with the nap schedule or would cause her to travel with the children in rush hours, she feels that this worker already understands her position to some extent. If the client is a working man, he responds favorably to the worker who suggests a late afternoon or an evening appointment.

2. *Privacy in interviews.* The place of the interview is important as a means of giving the client the sense that his confi-

dences are being respected and of giving the caseworker the opportunity to devote full and undivided attention to him. Privacy is the concrete manifestation of the agency's subscription to the principle of confidentiality.

3. *Care in keeping appointments.* A promptly kept appointment tells the client that he was expected and that the hour is his and only his. The pressures and emergencies in social agencies sometimes interfere with appointments; when this happens, something should be done to show the client that it could not be avoided. If the client has had to wait in a crowded room, recognition of this fact shows the worker's understanding of the client's probable discomfort. If the client had no appointment and was seen after a long wait, an interpretation of office procedures may help to stress the worker's interest in him as an individual.

4. *Preparation for interviews.* One of the best immediate preparations for individualizing the client is to review the written case record. The memory of details in the client's case is renewed and tentative specific purposes of the coming interview are planned. This preparation also helps the caseworker to shift into the background of his mind the other interests and responsibilities of the day, enabling him to focus more effectively upon this individual and his problem.

5. *Engaging the client.* If the client becomes engaged according to his present capacity in the study, diagnosis, and treatment, he will feel secure that he is being dealt with as an individual. As he participates in presenting the necessary data, he can also be helped to understand the reason for the data and the fact that the data are collected purposefully and in accordance with the client's problem or need. In the selection of treatment goals the client is aided to make his own choices and decisions. By refraining from unhealthy "doing for" the client when he can do something for himself, even in such mechanics as filling out forms, the social worker can manifest his conviction in the principle of individualization, and thus stimulate the client's self-confidence.

6. *Flexibility.* Although there is necessarily a certain degree of permanence to the purpose of each case, there is also some change calling for flexibility. The treatment goals need to be modified with the constantly increasing knowledge of the client and his situation and of the continuous developments and changes in the client's life. The ability to adjust goals and methods calls for mature judgment, objectivity, and skill in the caseworker. It is a specific way of individualizing the client.

ENDNOTES FOR PRINCIPLE I

1   Mary Willcox Glenn, "The Growth of Social Case Work in the United States." *The Family* 9:271, December 1928.
2   Robinson, *A Changing Psychology in Social Case Work,* p. 6.
3   *Ibid.,* p. 7.
4   Mary E. Richmond, *Social Diagnosis,* pp. 367-68. New York: Russell Sage Foundation, 1917.
5   Boethius, *Liber de persona et duabus naturis;* in *Patrologia Latina,* Vol. 64, col. 1343.
6   Mary J. McCormick, *Thomistic Philosophy in Social Casework,* p. 5. New York: Columbia University Press, 1948.
7   Hamilton, *Theory and Practice of Social Case Work,* p. 152.
8   *Ibid.,* p. 154.
9   Department of the Army, *Military Psychiatric Social Work,* p. 22. Washington: United States Government Printing Office, 1950.
10 *Ibid.,* p. 24.
11 Gordon Hamilton, "Helping People—The Growth of a Profession." *Journal of Social Casework* 29:296, October 1948.
12 Annette Garrett, *Interviewing: Its Principles and Methods,* p. 21. New York: Family Welfare Association of America, 1942.
13 Hamilton, "Helping People—The Growth of a Profession," p. 295.
14 *Differential Approach in Case Work Treatment,* p. 13 (discussion by Ruth Gartland of paper by Fern Lowry on "The Client's Needs as the Basis for Differential Approach in Treatment"). New York: Family Welfare Association of America, n. d.

Principle 2

PURPOSEFUL EXPRESSION

OF FEELINGS

MAN IS RATIONAL, having cognition and volition; and he is animal, having drives, impulses, senses, feelings, and emotions. These vital activities, rational, sentient, and vegetative, are interrelated and interdependent because man is a substantial unity.

Ideally, man is to govern himself by choosing the good and the true by the faculties of intellect and will, with the assistance of the well-ordered feelings and emotions of his sentient nature. The emotions are an integral part of man's nature, and their healthy development is necessary for the development of the total personality.

One of the greatest challenges in human living is to keep the emotions well ordered. In times of stress the emotions tend to seek domination of the person and his activities, countermanding

33

the dictates of good reason and urging the person to rule his life by the unreasonable demands of his animal and vegetative needs and drives. This could result in personality immaturity, in neurotic or psychotic illness, depending upon the depth and extent of the disordered emotions.

In the modern helping professions the importance of a well-ordered emotional life has been eminently recognized. Both psychology and psychiatry have studied the normal, healthy role of emotions in the personality structure, and they have made giant strides in the art of helping emotionally sick people to reorder their emotional lives. Social work has been enriched by the work of these professions. They have taught social work the interrelatedness of the emotional and the social components in human living. They have given social work a body of knowledge about human growth and development which has made the helping process of social work eminently more effective.

The basic psychological needs of man have been identified as the need for affection, security, status, expression, achievement, independence, and, possibly, novelty. Man's psychosocial needs are for participation or the sharing of experiences, for conformity to the pattern of the group, for social approval and recognition. If these needs are denied expression, frustration results. This is not to say that all frustration is harmful, for one of the marks of maturity is a certain capacity for frustration tolerance; but frustration may give rise to unhealthy mechanisms and undesirable behavior reactions.

While it is true that the degree of these needs varies from individual to individual, they are the needs of every man. Needs may be reinforced or inhibited, manifestations of the same need may be different, and men want much beyond their basic needs; the dynamics entering into the formation of each personality are unique.

The need for expression and for sharing experiences has been singled out by social workers as a very pertinent dynamic in the casework relationship. The importance of effectively recognizing this need in clients in every type of agency can be abundantly illustrated from the profession's literature. Two excerpts will suffice.

> . . . the interviewer has a responsibility to the applicant, which involves a skill of quick awareness, of sensitivity to the needs of the specific situation, and a warmth and understanding of the individual's need to express himself in his own way.[1]

> Since we deal with people in time of trouble, when they are "in the midst of emotions that come from the major catastrophes in life," it is important that we help them as they talk to us to express their emotions and that we try to understand the meaning which their problems have for them with a twofold purpose: First, that as they give expression to their feelings they may be relieved of pressures and tensions which have made the problem deeply disturbing. Thus, as they experience some change in feeling, they may be enabled better to bear the problem and cope with it more resourcefully and realistically. Second, through understanding the person's feeling we, as representatives of an assistance agency, may through thus sharing his problem afford each individual a relationship which strengthens him.[2]

This ingredient in the casework relationship has sometimes been referred to as "permissiveness." Since that term seems to need many qualifying phrases to be understood correctly, a more descriptive name is here adopted, "the purposeful expression of feelings," which can be described as follows:

> **Purposeful expression of feelings is the recognition of the client's need to express his feelings freely, especially his negative feelings. The caseworker listens purposefully, neither discouraging nor condemning the expression of these feelings, sometimes even actively stimulating and encouraging them when they are therapeutically useful as a part of the casework service.**

The client's expression of feelings is not expression for expression's sake, but for a purpose. It is directly related to his need for acceptance, to his need to be treated as an individual, to the help the client is seeking from the social agency, to the purpose of the client-worker relationship, and to his need to participate in the solution of his own problems.

THE EMOTIONAL COMPONENT IN SOCIAL PROBLEMS

A basic supposition in social casework practice is that the problem or need of every client is psychosocial; that is, every problem, even when the explicit request of the client is for a material form of assistance or a tangible service, has an emotional component.

Mr. S, for example, is applying for financial assistance. He has feelings about his economic indigence, thus making his problem a psychosocial one. He may feel like a failure; he may feel that his friends and relatives think less of him; he may feel that others are to blame for his present unfavorable circumstance.

Mr. and Mrs. T are requesting a temporary placement of their two children; they are asking for a tangible service. This need may have arisen because of a problem in housing, in health, in employment, or in marital conflict. It can validly be presumed that in making the request for placement they have some uncomfortable feelings, of greater or lesser depth, hidden or revealed in varying degrees. They may feel a sense of guilt, of failure as parents in not being able to take care of their children themselves. If they had tried unsuccessfully to place their children with relatives, they may have feelings of anger and resentment toward the relatives who did not help them in time of need. If they have no relatives, they may have a sense of social isolation because they must depend upon an agency rather than upon members of their own families.

The form which the feelings take may differ from client to client and vary in degree of intensity, but some variety of discomforting feelings are present in every client. The manifestation of the feelings may be gradual and spasmodic.

The caseworker's primary focus is the person in relation to his problem, rather than the problem alone. The total person with his problem comes to the agency for help; therefore effective casework must at least be aware of the feelings of the client about his problem. Not every case calls for an intensive treatment of these feelings; but every case must allow for the client's freedom to express his feelings in proportion to valid goals and purposes.

The client, as every person, is by nature a social being. He needs to be in communication with other human beings for the adequate growth and development of his total personality. He needs to communicate with another person to express his thoughts, attitudes, and feelings through some appropriate medium, whether through the spoken word or through a significant gesture or act. The need is especially felt when a person is in some kind of trouble or difficulty which intensifies the need for sharing the burden with another person. If a person with a problem is denied communication with others, some form of frustration results and the original problem becomes aggravated.

To deny a client the opportunity to express his feelings, his fears, his hopes, his hostility, is equivalent to a denial to deal with the total person. What the problem means to the client and how he feels about his problem are part of the problem, and in some cases may be the most difficult part of it.

PURPOSEFUL EXPRESSION

The client's expression of feelings should, of course, serve a valid purpose in the casework process. The specific purpose in each interview may be single or multiple; it may change from case to case, from interview to interview, and within the same interview. The following are some possible purposes.

1. One purpose may be to relieve pressures and tensions, and thus to help the client see his problem more clearly and objec-

tively. Feelings are expressed not just "to let off steam," but to free the client for positive, constructive action.

2. Another purpose may be to understand more adequately the problem and the person of the client for more accurate study, diagnosis, and treatment. The expressed feelings reveal what the problem means to the client, how he sees it, and give a deeper understanding of the "weight" that a client attaches to a certain problem or facet of a problem. It helps the caseworker form a more adequate evaluation of strengths and weaknesses.

3. Listening to a person's feelings in relation to a problem is a form of psychological support. The client feels that he has shared his problem in a real way with the caseworker, and thus his burden has been lessened because he and the caseworker are carrying it.

4. In some cases the negative feelings of the client may be the real problem. An expression of the feelings, then, brings them out into the open so that something can be done about them.

5. An important purpose may be to deepen the casework relationship. In some instances the caseworker, as a result of sensitive and accurate diagnostic thinking, may be aware that the client will soon be introducing for discussion intimate personal material, highly charged with emotional overtones. The caseworker may be aware that, for the effective treatment of that material when it will be introduced, the relationship needs to be stronger than it is at present. A deep relationship does not ordinarily happen suddenly; it must grow at an unforced pace, but its growth can be promoted by stimulating the expression of feelings that the client can comfortably and gradually express. The expression of feelings is a barometer of the depth of the relationship.

PURPOSEFUL LIMITATIONS

Free association is not a casework technique; from the very first interview, casework is focused upon the relation between the problem and the client, according to diagnostic thinking and treatment planning. The focus is upon the purpose. This focusing means giving the interviews a direction; and giving direction necessarily means operating within constructive limitations. The expression of feelings, likewise, must recognize constructive limitations which are aids in keeping a sense of direction in the interviews in order to promote the purpose of the casework helping process in each case. "Blowing off steam" can be irrelevant; it is irrelevant when it is not related to the purposes of the case.

In the early interviews of a case, when the real problem and the goals to be achieved are not clear, there may be less need to be aware of limitations to the expression of feelings. As the diagnosis and treatment goals become fairly well crystallized, however, the caseworker should approach each interview with long-range and immediate goals well in mind, and should focus the interview accordingly. This allows, of course, for the desired flexibility when issues arise which were not anticipated. Limitations help to keep interviews on a realistic basis.

The following are a few illustrations of limitations to the client's expression of feeling:

1. Agency function limits the expression of feelings to those which can be treated within the agency. It is obvious that in an agency which is not equipped to use intensive therapy in deeply disturbing emotional problems, the caseworker should not encourage the release of such intense feeling. In such an instance the caseworker should limit his help with feelings to the kind of service the agency is equipped to offer. The amount of time which a caseworker can give to a case, in relation to his total case load, is a limiting factor; it would be dangerous to encourage expressions of deep feelings when the caseworker knows that he cannot possibly do anything about them. For example, a caseworker in a public assistance agency with a caseload of two hundred would be unwise to encourage the expression of certain feelings, while a caseworker in another agency, with a caseload of twenty and with adequate psychiatric consultation available,

might very well do so. The former caseworker could, of course, refer the client to an appropriate community resource.

2. Caseworkers need to be cautious in the early interviews about the client's premature expression of deep feelings. A client might say too much too early, when he is really not ready for that depth of expression. A premature venting of feelings can create undesirable and unnecessary guilt feelings in the client; it can create obstacles in the relationship and cause purposeless hostility to the caseworker. Intake workers particularly need the skill to structure the interview in such a fashion that emotionally charged material will be kept at a minimum, in proportion to the purpose of the intake interview.

3. Although one of the valid purposes of the expression of feelings is psychological support, obtained through the client's sharing his burden with the caseworker, care needs to be had in preventing the client from putting the total burden upon the caseworker. The expression of feelings denotes a partial and temporarily necessary dependence of the client upon the caseworker, but it should not promote an overdependency.

4. In some instances the expression of feelings of hostility, possibly hostility to the worker or to the agency, can be an unhealthy attention-seeking device or a test of the caseworker's acceptance. Such behavior needs to be understood but not encouraged; exceptions, however, need to be recognized.

THE ROLE OF THE CASEWORKER

The function of the caseworker is principally to create an environment in which the client will be comfortable in giving expression to his feelings. The skill to create this environment is much more important than the skill of asking stimulating questions. In fact, the latter skill will be ineffective without the permissive atmosphere.

This desirable atmosphere is difficult to describe adequately, but some of its elements can be identified. In it the client feels that he can tell his story in his own way, that the caseworker considers the client's feelings important, that the caseworker is not uncomfortable when feelings are expressed, that the caseworker will not try to explain away the feelings in a facile, unrealistic way, that the caseworker will not condemn him for his negative feelings. The atmosphere includes the client's trust and confidence in the caseworker and the caseworker's acceptance of the client; it includes the caseworker's desire to help and the client's awareness of this attitude in the caseworker.

This atmosphere is not the exclusive creation of the caseworker. The caseworker is primarily responsible for it, but without the appropriate response and participation of the client it may neither come into being nor develop. The client brings to the casework situation his own personality and his attitudes toward himself and others, and his readiness to participate actively in a warm professional interpersonal relationship will be affected positively or adversely by his previous interpersonal relationships. Every client will need a period of testing the worker before he reveals his feelings; some clients will need more time, some less, and in some cases the worker may never pass the client's test. Many clients will express only superficial feelings until they are satisfied with the caseworker's attitude; at times a client may not find this satisfaction; other clients may express much emotion early in the relationship. Whatever the client's behavior, he will not reveal his true feelings until he is assured of the worker's permissive attitude; but sometimes a client will have an unreasonable need for this assurance.

Next in importance to a permissive atmosphere is the caseworker's real desire to help this individual. In the beginning of each new relationship this desire has more of an intellectual element, an awareness that this is a human being in trouble, asking and expecting help. As the relationship grows, this desire to help takes on more feeling tones; there is an understanding of the client and his problem on both an intellectual and emotional level, and a reaching out to him. This in no way means that the caseworker feels *like* the client, but rather feels *with* him. This real desire to help is not necessarily verbalized, but is conveyed to the client through feeling tones. When it is verbalized the warmth and feeling for the client is important, rather than what is said. Perhaps the caseworker may never say, "I want to help you," but somehow this attitude is communicated to the client on a feeling level. Even the most disturbed psychotic patients know whether the caseworker really wants to help. The catatonic schizophrenic upon recovery may tell of his awareness of attitudes toward him even though at the time he gave no indication of the awareness.

What can the caseworker do specifically to bring about the permissive atmosphere? There are no sure-fire methods, of course, because so much depends upon the self-awareness of the caseworker, the potential of the client, and that intangible equation between the caseworker and the client. However, a few suggestions are possible:

1. The caseworker should be relaxed in order to help the client feel fairly comfortable. This may be quite difficult on a busy day, but clearing one's desk helps to free one's mind of other pressures. The physical environment also has an effect upon both the client and the caseworker; a private interviewing room, comfortable chairs, and freedom from interruptions can help. The position of the caseworker's desk, a seemingly trivial detail, may also help; it could be so placed that the client can look out of the window or at a picture on the wall instead of having to look at the worker constantly.

2. Although good casework requires a certain amount of preparation for each interview, the foreground of the caseworker's mind should be relatively uncluttered with details. In as far as possible, these should be relegated to the background of the mind, so that the worker will be free to observe, to listen thoughtfully, and to think, see, and feel with the client. This will be possible only when the caseworker has made the preparation some time

prior to the interview. Just as students who have "crammed" for an examination frequently do not properly read and understand the examination questions, so also in "cramming" for an interview the caseworker may not see and understand the client. This calls for skill in the management of time.

3. Probably the most important element in creating the permissive attitude is the caseworker's ability to listen attentively and purposefully. When the worker gives his full attention the client feels his interest, sincerity, understanding, and objectivity, and this helps him to be more at ease and to talk more readily. The caseworker participates by making relevant comments and asking questions, since absence of response might be interpreted as disinterest; and when interruptions are made, they are made with a fully conscious purpose.

4. The caseworker may need to encourage the client to express his feelings. Even when provided with an atmosphere in which he feels free to express himself, the client frequently will not do so without help. How this encouragement is given is a matter of individual sensitivity and of the mode of expression and technique of each worker, but it must be geared to the individuality of each client. Although the internal attitude of the caseworker is more important than how it is done, some of the tools of encouraging the client are general questions, certainly not direct and threatening ones; the repetition of words or brief phrases which the client has used; directing comments to the feeling tones rather than to the facts presented; and by letting the client know, perhaps quite directly, that people do have strong ambivalent feelings about important persons and things in their environment, and that it is all right to express them within the casework relationship.

5. A sensitive awareness of the client's rate of movement, in each interview, toward his casework goals is very necessary. His motivation to work on his problem will be an indication of his need and desire to express feelings at any given time. Without sensitivity of his tempo the caseworker, although unaware of it,

may influence a slowing down or a speeding up of feeling expression, both of which may be harmful to the relationship.

6. Unrealistic reassurances, too early interpretation, and too much interpretation can block the client's expression of feelings. These are pitfalls into which a caseworker who tends to over-identify with a client is apt to stumble. Such a caseworker overestimates the anxiety of the client, underestimates his capacity to tolerate anxiety, and mistakenly rushes to relieve the client of the anxiety, thus cutting off the expression of feelings, which might have been the only effective way of actually relieving the anxiety.

EXPRESSION OF FEELINGS IN RELATION TO STUDY, DIAGNOSIS, AND TREATMENT

Feelings are facts. How a person feels about himself, about his interpersonal relationships, and about his problem is at least as important a part of the study as the objective facts of the situation. And the best source of knowledge as to how this particular individual feels about his problem is the client himself. The trend in contemporary casework practice, in many agencies, is toward limiting the use of collateral sources of information and toward spontaneous but focused and purposeful expression by the client himself. No one but the client can tell how he feels about his own problem; only he can tell the meaning of his own experience; his story is the first and most significant evidence in his history. Information received from the client in an interview in which he is permitted to present his problem as he sees it provides the data from which the caseworker formulates a diagnosis and comes to an understanding of the dynamics of the situation.

If the client is permitted to tell his story in his own way, to express his feelings about it, the caseworker gains invaluable material for the study. Gestures, smiles and other facial expressions, posture and behavior, are part of the totality of communication, as well as the verbal content. All of these are clues to his real feelings, his patterns of reaction and his defenses.

Until some feelings are released, it is frequently impossible to learn what the real problem is, and it is unlikely that the client will move toward a solution of his problem. If he is not free to dissipate some of these feelings by expressing them, he can never see his problem clearly, and it is unlikely that he will reveal enough of himself for the caseworker to have a clear picture. Frequently the client is so disturbed and so involved in his own problem that he cannot see it clearly until he has released some of his feelings. There must be enough release to relieve the constricting pressures that immobilize.

The expression of feelings aids diagnosis. Even though the diagnosis will be refined, added to, or changed, the caseworker begins at once to formulate some notion of the real nature of the problem. This formulation is based upon his knowledge of people generally and his knowledge of this person as he reveals himself in the casework relationship. The knowledge of this particular individual includes his ways of reacting to life situations, his own way of regarding his problems, his own attitude toward himself and others, his previous attempts to solve his problems, the quality and depth of his interpersonal relationships, his motivation for change, his idea of a solution to the present problem, and his capacities for solving his problem.

The diagnosis, in turn, can serve as a guide by indicating danger zones where expression of feelings needs to be avoided. For instance, when the diagnosis points to a psychosis, the release of feelings would be contraindicated. Similarly, the expression of feelings is dangerous in the case of a neurotic, whose feelings may relate to distant, long-repressed experiences. These may lead to areas in the client's past with which neither the client nor the caseworker is capable of coping. Diagnostic thinking will reveal whether the disturbing feeling is related to a recent or a distant experience; generally, the expression of feelings related to a fairly recent experience is apt to be more effective; the result may be dubious or even dangerous if the experience causing the feelings is more or less ancient. In such instances psychiatric consultations are indispensable.

Although it seems generally accepted that study, diagnosis, and treatment begin concurrently as soon as the client first enters the casework situation, treatment in its stricter sense may not begin, especially where the problem is predominantly emotional, until the relationship has a certain amount of depth. And the feelings expressed by the client are responsible for the depth and are a reliable gauge of it.

Moreover, the purposeful release of feelings is therapeutic in itself. Most persons have had the experience of feeling relief after expressing strong and disturbing emotions to a sympathetic friend; this kind of release, alone or combined with other forms of help, has a valid place in therapy. The value of expressing feelings is not only that it is a beneficial cathartic experience, but that it also prevents a possibly damaging repression.

Frequently the release of feelings removes the blind spots, and enables the client to see his problem more objectively and move toward a solution. His mind is somewhat freed of certain impediments and inhibitions, thereby enabling him to think more clearly, reason more accurately, and act more surely. Ordinarily a constricting emotional involvement rather than a lack of intelligence is at the base of the problem.

The expression of feelings brings them out into the open for discussion in the interview. Caseworkers are often aware of the presence of feelings with which the client really needs help, but they cannot discuss them or help the client to deal with them until the client feels free to talk about them. Once expressed by the client, the way is open to do something about them.

The expression of feelings, finally, is a dynamic in the client's participation in the solution of his own problem. If the client is not free to express his feelings but has the caseworker's own feelings and solutions imposed upon him, he is not active in his own problem. This kind of treatment usually has one of two effects.

neither of which is desirable: either the client fails to continue coming to the agency or he places the total responsibility upon the caseworker and becomes overly dependent. The client must involve himself in any real change, and feelings are part of the treatment in which he must involve himself. Acceptance by the worker of the client's hostile and negative feelings, moreover, conveys to him a feeling of worth as a person, which is a first step in motivation toward change and a solution.

ENDNOTES FOR PRINCIPLE 2

1 Helen R. Spitz, "The Interviewer's Responsibility in Determining Eligibility." *The Family* 21:122, June 1940.
2 Charlotte Towle, *Common Human Needs*, p. 9. New York: American Association of Social Workers, 1952.

Principle 3

CONTROLLED EMOTIONAL

INVOLVEMENT

EVERY communication is a two-way process. When one person speaks directly to another person, he expects some kind of a response; silence would indicate a disinterest in communication and, equivalently, a disinterest in the person.

The content of the communication indicates the kind of response that is expected. Generally speaking, the content can be classified into three categories: ideas only, feelings only, both ideas and feelings. When a person approaches the information desk at a railroad station and asks the clerk about the departure time of the next train for New York, he is communicating in ideas only. He is seeking information and is expecting a factual response. When an adult daughter, during the wake in a funeral parlor for her deceased mother, says to a relative, "It will be hard

48

to get used to the fact that mother is gone," she is communicating her feelings primarily. Only a feeling response would be appropriate. In casework interviews the content of the communication most often is a combination of thought and feeling. The nature of the content depends upon many things: the problem of the client, the function of the agency, the needs and feelings of the client in a particular interview, the changing moods of the client within an interview, and the purposes of the caseworker in the ongoing processes of study, diagnosis, and treatment.

In helping a client to establish his eligibility for public assistance, for instance, the caseworker needs to secure a certain amount of factual information. The content of the verbal communication in this phase of the study process will consist of ideas, of thoughts, of facts. However, even here the caseworker is sensitive to the feelings of the client.

Mrs. Brown brings her daughter, 8 years old, who is manifesting severe behavior problems, to a child-guidance clinic and says to the caseworker: "Sometimes I think I am to blame for Helen's problems. She came into the world with a quiet, happy disposition—she was such a sweet baby—and now look at her! Do you think I did something wrong?" Mrs. Brown is not just expressing her ideas; she is not just seeking information. She has tried to put into words a deep, painful feeling of her heart.

The social caseworker needs skill to communicate on both the thought and feeling levels. In order to help effectively when the content is factual the caseworker needs to be thoroughly familiar with the details of his own agency's policies and procedures and with the other available resources in the community. In order to help effectively when the content consists, partially or predominantly, of feelings the caseworker needs the skill to respond appropriately to the client's feelings. This is one of the most difficult skills in casework.

In this chapter the discussion of the caseworker's controlled emotional involvement is severely limited. It will be discussed as an element of the casework relationship. A more comprehensive discussion of it, as a technique in psychotherapy, would be far beyond the scope of this study.

This element of the casework relationship can be briefly described as follows:

The controlled emotional involvement is the caseworker's sensitivity to the client's feelings, an understanding of their meaning, and a purposeful, appropriate response to the client's feelings.

There are three components in the caseworker's controlled emotional involvement: sensitivity, understanding, and response. In actual practice they are necessarily and intimately interrelated, but for clarity in analysis they will be discussed separately.

SENSITIVITY

Essentially, sensitivity means seeing and listening to the feelings of the client.

Sometimes clients do not or cannot verbalize their feelings. This may happen most frequently in early interviews, when the client does not feel comfortable enough with the caseworker. It may happen because of the client's cultural or personality patterns, which frown upon external manifestation of feelings. Or the feelings may be so deep that they cannot, at that particular time, come to the surface to be expressed verbally. However, even though the client does not verbalize his feelings, he does manifest them in some visible or audible way. They may be manifested in his manner of speaking: the rate of speech, the hesitations, the overtones. They may be manifested by the total bearing: the face, the posture, the clothes, the use of the hands. These are clues and indices of the client's feelings.

The following excerpt from the Garcia case illustrates the sensitivity of the caseworker to the nonverbalized feelings of the client.[1] Easily visible manifestations of suppressed feelings often appear in the first interview. Even a beginning caseworker should be able to make these observations.

> Mrs. Garcia is an attractive woman who looked rather pale as she sat on the sofa. We explained that we were here to discuss their application for financial assistance and we knew a little of the family situation from Mr. Garcia, who had called at the office. Mrs. Garcia appeared nervous as evidenced in the rigid manner in which she sat buttoning and unbuttoning her sweater.
>
> Mr. Garcia came in shortly. He is of average height and slightly stout in build. After the introductions we noted that he seemed nervous and was unable to sit still. He has a very marked accent and does not speak English well. We said that we called at his home on Friday, the day he was at our office. He immediately told us he had an argument with the Employment Interviewer—the same information given us by his wife. When explaining this incident he spoke with a raised voice and gestured with his hands. After he finished talking he sat back breathing hard while his wife smiled at him.

In this recording the caseworker manifests awareness of Mr. and Mrs. Garcia's apprehensiveness and insecurity. Mrs. Garcia's nervous, rigid "buttoning and unbuttoning" of her sweater gave the caseworker an unmistakable clue to Mrs. Garcia's feelings. Mr. Garcia's "raised voice" and gestures revealed his inner feeling about his unpleasant argument with the employment interviewer. The intensity of his feelings was indicated by his "breathing hard." The caseworker also learned a great deal about the relationship between Mr. and Mrs. Garcia in noting that Mrs. Garcia smiled at her husband after he finished talking. By being sensitive to their nervous behavior and to their manner of speaking the caseworker became aware of the unspoken feelings of the clients.

An excerpt from the Brewster case illustrates the sensitivity of the caseworker in a more complicated situation.[2] The case involves the placement of Louise, 16 years old, in Burwick Hall, a boarding home. In an interview with Louise, her father, and her stepmother the caseworker records an awareness of unverbalized feelings in a difficult three-way relationship. It also shows the need of joining understanding to sensitivity.

Louise arrived out of breath and very white, asking for the ladies' room, saying that she had been nauseated and sick on the way. She thought it was because she was so tired and things were so unsettled. Then she went in and sat down with her parents, talking only with the stepmother and ignoring the father. She was most friendly with the stepmother, telling her that she could get her eggs and butter at a local store at a reduced rate. All three seemed somewhat embarrassed as to just where to start the conversation. I explained the Burwick Hall plan to Louise. She accepted this, I felt, without understanding too much about the plan, but accepting anything so that she would not have to live with the father and the stepmother. The father kept attempting, while I was explaining this, to drive me into a punishing role with Louise, telling her we would have to lay down the law to her, etc., and that she could not get by with what she had in the past. Louise did not seem to react in any way at this, nor did she look at her father. The stepmother did not fall into this, but was more concerned about whether Louise was really satisfied with this plan and expressed an interest in her being happy. . . .

The father then started telling Louise how she would have to mind in this home and do what I said. Also he hoped she would tell the truth. Louise looked at him defensively, and the father pointed out that Louise used to tell him wild tales . . . all of which turned out not to be true. I felt the father was putting me in a position of taking sides with either him or Louise as he went on talking, and rather than being placed in this position, I suggested they might like to talk among themselves for a while. The father said there was no need of this, that anything they had to say they could say in front of me. I left them alone, however, for about 15 minutes. When I returned Louise had been crying. The stepmother was assuring her that they wanted to help her, and her father was lecturing to her on how she must behave.

The caseworker evidently learned much about Louise's feelings from noting when the girl arrived that she was out of breath, very white, and in need of the ladies' room. The degree of her dread of the interview was confirmed by her statement that she was nauseated and sick on the way to the agency. Louise's positive feelings toward her stepmother were indicated by her friendliness to her. Louise's negative feelings toward her father were painfully evident; she neither looked at him nor talked to him, except to glance at him defensively when he lectured to her about lying. The father's feelings toward Louise were manifested by his repeated insistence that she needed to be obedient and truthful. From this sensitive observation the caseworker was able to make a tentative evaluation of the relationships, an important item for the treatment plan in this case. Subsequent interviews would either confirm or alter this evaluation.

Sometimes clients give verbal expression to their feelings. In the Sanca case Mrs. Sanca tells how she feels in a very direct way.[3]

When she came into the interviewing room she immediately said that she was feeling very upset. I asked what she felt was bothering her. She didn't know, but realized she was all excited and it just seemed to be everything. I asked if she could give some specific example of what she meant. She then told me that she thought it was just a pile up of everything that had happened. She and her husband have had one problem after another since they were married and now that things are a little more quiet, she seems to be having a reaction.

She said in a rather discouraged tone that she hadn't worked for a week now and she wasn't feeling any better. I said that apparently all this had been piling up for a long time and it would take quite some period before she would feel like her old self again but that she shouldn't be discouraged because she hasn't had an immediate recovery. Mrs. S put her hands to her head and said "I don't know why I'm so upset." I asked if she had noticed when she seemed to feel most nervous. She knew the children got on her nerves, that they seemed to get her all excited and that there is so much to do, that she's always working and never seems to get things done, which causes her to feel all tense inside. I asked if she had noticed this feeling at any other time. She again put her head in her hands and said "No, I don't know what it is. I can't sleep nights. I dream people are fighting and then I wake up all upset." Even fights in the neighborhood disturb her, so that she just has to go and sit down for a while.

Mrs. Sanca's verbalization of her confusion and emotional depression gave an indication of her feelings. The factual information was vague and indefinite, but the feeling tones were informative. They afforded the caseworker an entrance into the client's emotional condition which, depending upon further data and sound diagnostic thinking, could be explored further in subsequent interviews.

Sensitivity to the feelings of clients comes as a result of many things. It begins with the caseworker's real conviction about the importance of feelings in the client's life. It is developed only at the price of critical examination of practice, benefiting from experience, supervision, and self-discipline. As any other professional skill, it is developed gradually, proceeding slowly from the simple to the more complex.

The self-discipline of the caseworker relates to an awareness of the caseworker's own needs and feelings, so that they do not block his sensitivity. It means that the caseworker learns to manage his own train of thought in an interview in such a way that it does not deafen nor blind him to the client's feelings. Concretely, it means a good management of a case load, so that distracting concerns are kept to a minimum and so that the case-worker can be relaxed enough to listen.

UNDERSTANDING

As a professional helping person, the caseworker needs to understand the meaning of the feelings in relation to the client and his problems. He needs to know what he is doing, what is going on, when he stimulates the client to express his feel-ings, and how this expression is contributing to the goals in the case. The understanding is a continuous process; in each interview the understanding should increase and grow, but in many cases the caseworker may have to be satisfied temporarily with a partial understanding and continue to strive toward a fuller understanding.

Knowledge of human behavior is indispensable for under-standing the meaning of feelings. This knowledge comes from psychology, psychiatry, and other social sciences, it comes from introspection upon one's own life experiences and from profes-sional practice. It includes a knowledge of common human needs, of patterns of human reactions and defenses in times of stress. This general knowledge is then used as a framework within which this particular client, with his individual and unique qual-ities, can be better understood and helped. It helps the caseworker to learn what the client's feelings mean to him. An unfortunate experience for one person may result in an entirely different re-sponse or pattern of feeling responses for another person. The aim of the caseworker is to understand what these feelings mean to this client. Individualization also helps in seeing the inter-relatedness of the emotional with environmental components of the client's problem.

Each caseworker must seek his own aids in developing skill in understanding the meaning of feelings. The use of supervision and psychiatric consultation are big aids. The practice of making conjectures about the various possible meanings of the feelings expressed by the client, together with a periodical examination and evaluation of the conjectures in the light of the movement in the case, is a very valuable device.

The caseworker in the Brewster case briefly and simply records her understanding of the feelings expressed by Louise in the first interview. The girl, for whom a boarding home placement was arranged, manifested strong negative feelings toward her father, and verbalized affection for her natural mother who deserted her, but her real feelings were the exact opposite.

> My impression in this interview was that Louise's independence and rational discussion of her situation are strong defenses against the real dependency needs of a very lonely and badly hurt girl. I felt her hostility toward her father was an indication of her strong attachment to him. Basically she has much hostility toward her mother for deserting her and has turned it into an outward expression of devotion to her. I do not feel that Louise will be able to accept a foster home until some of these feelings are worked through with her. Since she really has no place to live, I feel that it is advisable for her to stay in the agency's temporary receiving home as a group placement will probably be better for her at least for the time being.

It was obvious to the caseworker that Louise's feelings toward her parents constituted a real problem, with which she would need extensive casework help. The seriousness of the girl's unsatisfactory relationship with her parents was seen in her real loneliness and dependence, which she attempted to conceal by means of external mannerisms of independence and self-sufficiency. She expressed hostility for her father, while probably having a strong attachment to him. And she expressed devotion for her natural mother, while there were valid indications that she harbored much hostility toward her. As the case developed, these first impressions of the caseworker were confirmed. If the caseworker had not understood the real meaning of the feelings expressed by

Louise, which were actually the very opposite of their literal and surface meaning, the caseworker would have considerably reduced her effectiveness in helping the client. The response to the feelings would have been seriously misdirected, and the caseworker's relationship with the girl would have had a quality of unreality.

The caseworker had weekly interviews with Louise Brewster for about three months, at which time the case was presented for staff discussion. The following excerpt illustrates the value of this aid for increasing the caseworker's understanding of the client's feelings and for relating this understanding to the relationship and to treatment goals.

> The group felt that Louise had a strong ego with good integration. They were somewhat concerned about the extent to which she repressed feelings but felt this wasn't serious as it was breaking through and that continued acceptance by the caseworker should help her in expressing her emotions. They felt that the worker should continue to be friendly with her, giving her an opportunity to discuss her past and to express considerable interest in present and future plans for her, that the worker at the present time was regarded more as a friend but that Louise's transference was gradually to use the worker as a mother figure. The psychiatrist felt that as this relationship became stronger Louise would work out many of her problems. The psychiatrist also emphasized that Louise's inability to accept a foster home was complicated in that she was rejected not only by the adoptive mother but by her own mother and she felt it was questionable that she would ever be able to take a foster home placement. Placement at the "Y" and at Burwick Hall were discussed and the general feeling was that Burwick Hall would be a better placement for Louise since the "Y" would force her into a mature role. The goal should be to encourage her to be more like a girl of 17 than the adult she now acts. It was suggested not to point out too rapidly anything against her mother, as this would be siding with her father, forcing Louise to take sides against the worker. The psychiatrist felt that this girl should be encour-

aged to go on to college if possible. She has the type of personality to go through on scholarship and borrow money and that she probably would prefer to do it this way.

Through this staffing the caseworker confirmed and refined many of the conjectures and hypotheses which she formulated in previous interviews. This also provided her with two clear directions for subsequent interviews: (1) to continue to accept and encourage Louise to express her feelings about her parents, which she had previously repressed; (2) to allow the friend-friend quality in the relationship to continue for a while, but to expect it to develop qualities of a mother-daughter relationship, through which Louise would be able to work out many of her feelings toward her mother. The over-all estimate of Louise's strengths were likewise confirmed: she had a strong ego with good integration and a potential for college work.

RESPONSE

Sensitivity and understanding are insufficient in themselves; they are means to the response. The caseworker's response to the client on the feeling level is the most important psychological element in the casework relationship, and it is perhaps the most difficult of the casework skills. It frightens the beginning caseworker; it frequently mystifies and always intrigues the experienced practitioner because the response is individualized to each client and even to the changing moods of the client within a single interview.

This needs stressing: the response is not necessarily verbal. Essentially it is a response of attitude and feeling, guided by knowledge and purpose. It is primarily an internal response, wherein the caseworker consciously and purposefully identifies with the feelings of the client. It is a sharing in the client's feelings; not the sharing of a relative in another relative's grief, but the sharing of a warmly human professional person with fine sensitivities in the feelings of another human being who is in need of assistance.

Although the response is primarily internal, it is communicated to the client through some form of external manifestation, whether of word, of facial expression, of tone of speech, or of action. The external form is relatively unimportant. That there be some kind of response is very important, for the client needs to be aware of it. If the caseworker has a desirable internal response, normally the externalization will take care of itself. Therefore, in the development of the caseworker's skill in this area, more attention needs to be given to the growth of internal feeling responses than to the specific way of externalizing it. The response has meaning only in proportion to how thoroughly it comes "from the heart." Phrases such as "I know how you feel," "This must be very hard on you," and so forth, will be ineffective unless they spring from within. Instinctively at least the client can detect the emptiness of words only.

Whether or not, at a given time in a given interview, the caseworker should verbalize his response is too individual a thing to generalize about. Experienced caseworkers know that, on occasion, they can say absolutely nothing and feel sure that, because of their internal disposition of attitudes and feelings, the client senses the internal response. The caseworker's educated intuition is sometimes the only guide that can indicate whether the response should or should not be verbalized. Examining in retrospect the wisdom of verbalizing or not verbalizing is one way of educating the intuition.

In making a verbal response to feeling content, purposefulness and selectivity are most important. Obviously, the caseworker does not respond verbally to every expression of feelings about many people or things. It must be a selective response which is guided by purpose, including the over-all purpose of the case, the purpose of this particular interview, and the immediate purpose of the response.

The immediate purpose may be to give the client psychological support by expressing acceptance and by a sympathetic listening to and understanding of the client's troubles. It may be to strengthen the client's security in expressing his feelings to the worker. It may be to help the client to manifest progressively deeper feelings and to encourage further expression. In some instances, especially if the expression of deeper feelings would be premature or beyond the scope of the caseworker's service, the purpose may be the opposite: to help prevent the client from going deeper and to help him focus on the feelings just expressed. Clarification of feelings is another possible purpose. Whatever the caseworker's immediate purpose may be—and the possibilities are numerous—the response is never static. The caseworker should strive to make responses consciously and deliberately with a known purpose in mind. At times, of course, the caseworker may have to rely upon intuitive responses, with only a vague consciousness of purpose.

ILLUSTRATION OF RESPONSE

Mrs. Sanca, 36 years old, was seeking casework help for herself. She was having nervous reactions from a series of health problems suffered by her husband and her 5-year-old daughter. In the first interview she narrated with feeling that she was "all tense inside," "upset," and that she could not sleep. She vaguely hinted at irritations arising from her children and her neighbors. The following comment of the caseworker was intended to give Mrs. Sanca a beginning acceptance, an assurance of help, and to get at some specifics for the study process.

> I said I thought we could work this out together but I would need to know more about how she felt and what had happened to her, before I could really be of much help. I asked if she could tell me something about her earlier life. Mrs. S responded to this very quickly.

When she was 5 years old, she was boarded with her grand-mother, who beat her frequently, did not allow her to play, and made her work constantly. Rebellion brought only more beatings. The caseworker asked if she saw her parents during this time.

> She said that they lived only a couple of blocks away but the only time she saw them was when she sneaked up there. I purposely did not go into her feelings about this at this time.

The caseworker's purposeful refraining from stimulating ex-pression of feelings about the parents of Mrs. Sanca is worth noting. The recording does not contain the caseworker's reason for this, but a few possible reasons can be conjectured. Since Mrs. Sanca's negative feelings about her grandmother were so intense and so bitter, and since she indicated similar feelings about her parents, a fuller expression of these feelings might be too much for a first interview. Moreover, the caseworker may have wanted at this time more factual information about Mrs. Sanca.

She then narrated that she met her future husband when she was 17, that he was a student at the university, that he suffered from ulcers, and that her father at first disapproved of him very strongly. After five years of courtship they were married. Im-mediately after their marriage her husband was hospitalized and was unemployed for about a year, and their daughter was born with a dislocated hip.

The following response of the caseworker was intended to draw out both feeling and factual content, while verbalizing sympathetic understanding.

> I asked if there was any period in her married life when things seemed to go pretty well. Mrs. S said, "Oh, no, there was always something." I asked about her husband during all this time. She said immediately, "Oh, he is a very good man. He has always stayed at home with me, doesn't gamble or drink, and is really very good." I said these were certainly very important factors

but I wondered if there was something which she hadn't found too satisfying, and which was upsetting to her. She had gone to work to help him out but he had never helped her with the responsibilities at home. She said in a very discouraged manner, "I had to do everything at home." I said I knew this had made it hard. Her husband has been better recently, because he seems to realize that she is quite upset. I repeated that she is now at home, has more time to do her housework, and also her husband is helping her. I said I was glad of this because I felt she apparently had carried a great deal for a long time.

The day before the second interview Mrs. Sanca's two children left for a nursery camp operated by the agency. She had expected a phone call about the children from the caseworker the night before, but the caseworker had not phoned until the following noon. The caseworker's simple and frank response to Mrs. Sanca's disappointment is worth noting.

She expressed some resentment to me, saying that she had understood I would call last night. I said I could see how she might feel I had let her down and I was sorry there had been this misunderstanding. Mrs. S said it was all right.

Since Mrs. Sanca indicated some disproportionate concern about the children at camp, the caseworker attempted to stimulate Mrs. Sanca's expression of feelings and thus to help clarify her attitudes in this regard. The following excerpt illustrates a series of easy, natural responses.

I said it must be a funny feeling, in a way; to know the children can get along when they are away from home. Mrs. S then began to talk about how worried she had been Sunday night and how the children had seemed so excited. I asked just how she had felt. She didn't know whether they would be happy and the first day they were gone she didn't know what to do with herself. She hadn't gotten any housework done and had just sat around. She repeated she was worried about the children. I said that mothers often found the first separation hard, for it wasn't easy suddenly to find they are no longer babies. She said this was true, but after she heard from me, she whipped through her housework in no time. She said it was a wonderful feeling to be able to leave the house this afternoon and not have to make plans for the children. I said I was glad to hear she was having times when she felt that way, but perhaps there would be some feelings of both pleasure and restlessness.

One of the treatment goals in this case, suggested to the worker in a previous psychiatric consultation, was to help Mrs. Sanca to free herself from her fear of her grandmother and mother, which originated in her childhood. As an adult she continued to have behavior patterns of rigidly conforming to what she thought they approved and demanded. The caseworker's response in the following excerpt is directed to helping Mrs. Sanca develop some insight into this.

There was a silence in which Mrs. S seemed to be gathering up her courage. She then said, "Mrs. Hull, I went to see my mother Saturday and told her I couldn't give her any more money because I am not working." I said I knew this hadn't been easy for her to do and I wondered how she had felt before and after. Mrs. S said, "Do you know what my mother said? She said she had wondered how I could possibly pay her when I wasn't working and that it was all right." I asked how she had felt when her mother said this. She had felt relieved and if it hadn't been for me she never could have done it. I said, "So you had worried and you hadn't needed to." She said, "I always do that. I worry and worry about what people will think." . . . I said from what she told me her grandmother was frequently mad, but most people aren't like her grandmother. Mrs. S said, "That's true. I still dream about her and think she will beat me up." I said her mother knew she couldn't afford to pay her now and had understood this. Mrs. S described how she had spent the entire week getting up enough courage to tell her mother about the money and now she knew she had been silly. I said I thought the important thing was that she had been able to risk telling her mother and maybe she could try this sort of thing again.

The caseworker was dealing with this obvious transference by discussing it in terms of concrete situational factors rather than in theoretical terms.

The termination of this second interview illustrates responses which give support to the client by repeating the caseworker's desire to help, and by pointing out realistically that progress in her emotional improvement will have its ups and downs.

Mrs. S was silent and then said, "Why do I get so upset some days?" One day the previous week she had been so nervous she had thought of calling the doctor, but she hadn't. I said that finding out why she got so upset was something we could try to learn together. Mrs. S said, "I think I worry too much—actually, things aren't as bad as I expect." I smiled and said, "No, I don't think they are but there is still that feeling inside." She said, "It's funny, isn't it?" I nodded and then told Mrs. S I would like to see her again next week and if in the meantime she wanted to get in touch with me she should feel free to. I again told her how good I thought it was that she had told her mother. I also said she shouldn't expect a great change in her feelings just because the children were away and she could rest, because for some people it is easier to be busy. "I think that's right, but why did I get so nervous when I was working?" I said that sometimes we can do too much, but right now not doing anything was a great change. Mrs. S said, "That's right. I guess it will take me a while to get used to it." I nodded and said I would see her again next week when we could discuss things further.

In the third interview Mrs. Sanca said that she felt better all week, but over the week end she was very upset. The caseworker thought that Mrs. Sanca needed a little stimulation to talk about herself in more concrete terms and posed a brief question which gave Mrs. Sanca an opportunity to be more specific. It was not a probing question, and Mrs. Sanca was left free to avoid the question or to delve deeper into her feelings if she was ready to do so.

> Saturday night she had not been able to go to sleep for several hours, and had just lain in bed shaking. Her husband asked what was the matter but she did not want to tell him. All kinds of things were going through her mind, and she became more and more tense as she lay there. I said questioningly "All kinds of things?" I felt Mrs. S was reluctant to really say what she had been thinking about in concrete terms, so instead said the children had gotten her all upset when they came home. I said that children can be very upsetting at times and that all parents had periods when their children upset them, as well as periods when they enjoyed their children very much. Mrs. S looked at me for a minute and said, "That's true, isn't it," and then began to laugh in a rather pleased manner. I said, "Yes, children certainly can be irritating sometimes."

The caseworker may have suspected that there was some conflict in the relationship between husband and wife; but if there was, Mrs. Sanca evidently was not ready to talk about it and continued to focus upon her children.

The next excerpt illustrates a response to a direct question from the client, in which the caseworker gives support and expresses acceptance and optimism in a realistic way.

> Mrs. S broke into her own description by saying, "Mrs. Hull, why do you suppose I was so upset Saturday night? It was just awful." I asked if she had had nights like this before. Before her children went to camp she had not been able to get any sleep. I said actually she had had many years when she had to drive herself in order to keep things going. I reviewed the fact that her husband had been out of work for a long time, had fre-

quently been ill, and that Cynthia had been sick for such a long period. I said through all this she had carried on and kept things going very well, but that it would take a lot out of anyone, and would leave them pretty keyed up. I thought she was still having a reaction from all this. I said I really thought it was very encouraging that she had been able to relax during the time they were away, but the period hadn't been long enough. I explained that she would probably find she had these upset periods off and on for quite a while, but the fact that she had gone for a week or so without one was very encouraging. "You know it took a long time for all this to build up and it's going to take quite a while for it to subside again." Mrs. S said, "Yes, that's true."

These excerpts from the first three interviews of the Sanca case, in which there was a total of sixteen interviews, illustrate in a simple form that element of the casework relationship which we have chosen to call "controlled emotional involvement." Since the client's problem was principally in the emotional area, the caseworker stimulated the client to talk out her feelings. The caseworker became "involved" emotionally by responding to the feelings. This involvement was "controlled," that is, directed by the over-all purpose of the case, by the client's changing needs in each interview and by the caseworker's ongoing diagnostic thinking.

ENDNOTES FOR PRINCIPLE 3

1 *Garcia Record* (mimeographed). New York: Council on Social Work Education, n. d.
2 *Brewster Record* (mimeographed). New York: Council on Social Work Education, n. d.
3 *Sanca* (mimeographed). New York: Family Service Association of America, 1952.

Principle 4

ACCEPTANCE

IN 1929 the report of the Milford Conference noted that the actual practice of social casework was more precise than the terminology, the principles, and the philosophy underlying its practice. It was felt that this situation had to be remedied if social casework was to develop.[1] In 1949 the lack of definitive concepts and precise terminology was again pointed up as creating misunderstandings and barriers which limited social work education and training and hindered communication with other professions.[2]

One of the most commonly used terms in social work is "acceptance." Everyone seems to agree upon its importance, especially as it is lived by the caseworker in the relationship with the client, but it remains one of the vaguest terms in our professional language.

67

Etymologically the word "accept" has different shades of meaning when referring to an inanimate thing, to an intellectual concept, or to a person. Referring to a thing, to accept means to receive, as to accept a gift. Referring to an intellectual concept, to accept means "to recognize as true and/or significant" or "to engage oneself by a favorable reply to," as in accepting the concept of democracy as a good form of government. In referring to a person, to accept means to treat with respect.

In the literature of social work no formal analysis or definition of the term is to be found; a few writers explain the term, but never in more than a short paragraph. Some illustrations of these explanations are here presented in chronological order; they were helpful in the definition formulated in this chapter.

1932 We "accept" him [the client] when we are able to understand him as he is, and to respect his integrity as a fellow human being.[3]

1947 "Acceptance" is a term widely used to describe the caseworker's attitude toward his client. It embraces two basic ideas—one negative and one positive. (1) The caseworker must not condemn or feel hostile toward a client because of his behavior no matter how greatly it may differ from behavior of which he personally would approve. (2) In order to help a client the caseworker must feel genuine warmth, a certain "outgoingness" to the other person to form a bridge across which help may be given. He must really want to add something to the comfort and happiness of the other person, not for the satisfaction of a successful case (although this feeling may also be present) nor primarily for the benefit of society but because he really cares what happens to this particular individual.[4]

1950 It [social casework] accepts the individual—such as he is and with all his limitations—as he is expected to learn to accept others, without prejudice. Not out of personal friendship but as a quality of life, it offers warmth, acceptance, and understanding, in quiet illustration of a quality in human relations that might have value everywhere.[5]

1951 Interviewing skill rests on a fundamental professional attitude called "acceptance." This means acceptance of the other person as he is—in whatever situation, no matter how unpleasant or uncongenial to the interviewer, with whatever behavior, aggressiveness, hostility, dependency, or lack of frankness he may manifest. This attitude can come only from respect for people and a genuine desire to help anyone who is in need or trouble. It is translated through courtesy, patience, willingness to listen, and not being critical or disapproving of whatever the client may complain of, request, or reveal about himself.[6]

. . . the fundamental attitude required from the therapist is one of complete *understanding*. . . . It means accepting the patient in the sense of *not reacting against* or *attacking* or *criticizing* the person as he actually is, and it means also *fully* accepting his real potentialities and possibilities. It means accepting what he is as *a possible starting-point of new growth*.[7]

1954 The "central dynamic" in this giving of help and strength is . . . a "special kind of love" called "acceptance," a love which "consists of warmth, concern, therapeutic understanding, interest in helping the person to get well," that is, to regain control of his own life and conduct. This "love" is further characterized by a "consistent neutrality and firmness" which make it a sincere expression of the caseworker's willingness "consciously to enter and share in" the life experiences of another.[8]

The principle of acceptance implies that social workers must perceive, acknowledge, receive, and establish a relationship with the individual client as he actually is, not as we wish him to be or think he should be. It means that no matter how much the client may have distorted reality, no matter how much our perception of it may differ from his, or how greatly our values may differ from his, we must acknowledge and accept him as he is if we are to help him. This does not mean that we do not hope to effect change in him, but rather that the art of helping, like any other art, depends on accepting the material with which we propose to work as it actually exists, with its limitations as well as its potentialities. This principle could be restated by saying that in social work one begins where the client is and, at every stage in the helping process, relates oneself to the client as he is at each given moment.[9]

In the above quotations acceptance has been called "a quality of life," "a professional attitude," "a fundamental attitude," "the central dynamic," and a "principle." It would seem that, in reference to the caseworker's internal disposition before that internal disposition has been put into action, acceptance should be called an attitude: a volitional direction based upon an intellectual conviction and in some instances colored with an emotion. As a professed rule of action or conduct resulting from a consciously adopted attitude it is more properly called a principle.

The action of acceptance was indicated as therapeutic understanding, respecting, loving, perceiving, acknowledging, helping, and receiving. It would seem that there are three steps in the action of acceptance: (1) *perceiving;* the caseworker must first see and see objectively what he is accepting; (2) *therapeutic understanding;* the caseworker must see the object of acceptance in relation to the causes which brought about the object, in relation to what it means to this person, and in relation to the purpose of the casework process in each individual case; and (3) *acknowledging* it as a pertinent reality.

The object of acceptance, the "what" of acceptance, was stated in the quotations given on the previous pages as follows: "his integrity as a fellow human being," "the individual as he is, with all his limitations," "as he is, regardless of unpleasant or uncongenial attitudes or behavior," "his real potentialities," and "the individual client as he actually is, not as we wish him to be or think he should be." All these expressions, it seems, can be summarized by saying that the object of acceptance is the individual client as he actually is, with his strengths and weaknesses, his potentialities and limitations, his congenial and uncongenial attitudes, his positive and negative feelings, his acceptable and unacceptable behavior. The extremely vital point is that the case-worker, while seeing the client's negatives realistically, maintains an equally real respect for him.

The qualities of acceptance as contained in the same quotations are "warmth," "courtesy," "listening," "respect," "a certain outgoingness," "concern," "interest," "consistent maturity and firmness," and "willingness consciously to enter and share in the life experience of another."

The purpose of acceptance was said to be "to respect his integrity as a fellow human being," "to help [the person] in need or trouble," "to add something to the comfort and happiness of the other person," and "in helping the person to get well . . . to regain control of his own life and conduct." The purpose of acceptance in casework, all seem to agree, is therapeutic: to help the client with his problems and needs. It differs, therefore, from acceptance in other interpersonal relationships, such as the acceptance of a social companion or a professional colleague.

One additional point needs to be made: accepting the client as he is, with deviant attitudes, principles, or behavior, obviously does not mean concurrence with or approval of the deviancy. Acceptance of these means perceiving, therapeutic understanding, and acknowledging them as a part of reality, but not as true and good. The difference between accepting and approving has been abundantly recognized by social workers.

> Social workers cannot and should not be impartial in the face of individual and social misery and evil. The place of value judgments is always assumed, but they do not take the conventional form of praising or blaming the person who is to be helped.[10]

> The patient will not be helped if he finds that the antisocial behavior for which he was sent for psychiatric evaluation is apparently approved of by the social worker. The nonjudgmental attitude in such a case should transmit to the patient the concept that his behavior is neither being praised nor condemned, but is

being studied objectively in order that he can be understood and helped with his difficulty. It is necessary to accept the patient as a person who deserves and needs help, but it is not necessary to accept his behavior.[11]

Of course, this acceptance on the part of the worker does not mean that he makes the person's problem and values his very own. That would be impossible and undesirable. In fact, it is always necessary and important for the worker to maintain professional standards.[12]

It is the responsibility of the profession to see that acceptance of the person does not become confused with acceptance of immoral or antisocial deeds.[13]

On the basis of the foregoing discussion, therefore, the following definition of acceptance is offered:

Acceptance is a principle of action wherein the caseworker perceives and deals with the client as he really is, including his strengths and weaknesses, his congenial and uncongenial qualities, his positive and negative feelings, his constructive and destructive attitudes and behavior, maintaining all the while a sense of the client's innate dignity and personal worth.

Acceptance does not mean approval of deviant attitudes or behavior. The object of acceptance is not "the good" but "the real." The object of acceptance is pertinent reality.

The purpose of acceptance is therapeutic: to aid the caseworker in understanding the client as he really is, thus making casework more effective; and to help the client free himself from undesirable defenses, so that he feels safe to reveal himself and look at himself as he really is, and thus to deal with his problem and himself in a more realistic way.

The human person has intrinsic value. He has an innate dignity and worth, basic rights and needs. Man has a unique value in the universe. This intrinsic value is derived from God, his Creator, and is not affected by personal success or failure in things physical, economic, social, or anything else. The applicant for financial assistance, the deserted child, the alcoholic lying at the rear door of a tavern on Skid Row, the violent patient in a mental hospital, each has the same intrinsic human dignity and value as the wealthy person, the child of loving parents, the well-integrated person, and even the saint. The social failures, just as the socially successful, are made in the image of God, are children of the infinitely loving heavenly Father and heirs of heaven.

> We can say of this concept of human dignity that it is a philosophical bastion of the free world. For nearly a hundred years Dialectical Materialism has been expanding, until, here in the mid-twentieth century, it has virtually encircled us. In practice, the dignity of the human being is the single most important concept that stands between us and engulfment. It is this idea—or at any rate, what it stands for—that has given meaning to our policies, other than that of a mere struggle for power; it is this that has caused us to lay down our lives to block the encroachments of totalitarians like Mussolini and Hitler; and it is this that gives us the courage and the will to call the bluffs and oppose the maneuvers of the Kremlin.[14]

No individual characteristic forfeits this value. Heredity and environment do not alter a person's basic value. Even unacceptable acts, such as violations of the civil law or of the moral law, do not deprive the person of his fundamental God-given dignity. In behavior which constitutes a violation of the will of God man is not acting in conformity with his dignity, but he does not lose his dignity thereby.

It is necessary to stress the source of human dignity. It does not come from personal success; it does not originate in a Bill of

Rights or in a democratic Constitution—these merely proclaim the worth of the individual rather than bestow it. The origin of the dignity of humanity is divinity.

> The very *rationale* of his dignity . . . consists in a relation to his Creator which constitutes him as *imago Dei,* as the image of God in nature and the imitative parallel in operation. Man is the image of God in his mind, and then in his will, and in the operation of these faculties in knowing and loving. He images God in all their operations, but eminently so when he pursues with them the same object as God, which is God Himself. He is not only intelligent, as God, and able freely to love, as God does, but by those very powers, can direct his rational energies upon God directly and expend his divine-like powers upon precisely the same infinite object upon which intelligence and love itself directs His infinite energy. This re-presentation, as it were, of the nature and activity of God upon earth constitutes man in a worth and dignity which from its very nature is evidently comparable and measurable only by the standard and rule which is the infinite God Himself, and man's dignity is something of an incarnation of the Creator in creation, in man's measure, but with a divine model.[15]

Because of its origin the person cannot be deprived of his worth by anything or anyone. Man's worth is inalienable. This value of the human person is the basis for the principle of acceptance and gives meaning and direction to the casework helping process.

> Human persons must again be seen as *human,* in meanings they have forgotten "human" had. And the human must be seen in a certain measure and manner, as *divine.* Men must not be approached as animals. We face each other as intelligent images of God. Our native rational appreciation of the God-model whose image we are, our native love of what is like us, and our natural recognition of the value and dignity of both our God

and His divine images around us in men, must prompt us once more to approach our God, and almost also our fellow man— upon our knees.[16]

THE NEED OF THE CLIENT

The client who comes to the social agency with a problem is essentially a person who is dissatisfied with some aspect of his present living, sees the need for change, but cannot make the change unaided due to environmental pressures or limitations within his personality. He is not happy about himself; or rather, he is ambivalent about himself. On the one hand he is somewhat aware, in an individual manner, of his weaknesses and failures; while on the other hand he has a sense of his own dignity and worth as a person. The strength of the desire for change and the readiness to effect change exist in varying degrees in each individual. When he seeks help because he is unable to cope with his own problems, a constellation of feelings and attitudes, which are a part of his adjustment mechanism, become activated in a unique way.

His ambivalence extends to the caseworker: he realizes that he must reveal some of his shortcomings to the caseworker in order to be helped, while at the same time he fears that the caseworker, seeing him as he is, may think less of him as a person. He fears disapproval. This fear may cause any one of a number of reactions, depending on the nature of the problem and the personality of the client. He feels the insecurity of approaching someone he has never met; he may fear that his request for help will be refused; he may feel resentment against the conditions that make it necessary for him to seek help; and he may fear the self-involvement with the caseworker. Therefore he constructs defenses, behind which he tries to hide a part of himself. He feels that it is unsafe for him to manifest some things which he knows need to be manifested because they are pertinent to his problem. He has buried some things so deeply that he is aware of them only vaguely; the fear of what is hidden may be worse than the reality itself.

Because it is so possible that the client may be protecting himself against many of his own unacceptable feelings, which may be intimately related to the problem, it becomes important that an accepting atmosphere be created in which the need to protect himself becomes lessened.

Haltingly, he may begin to reveal negative feelings toward persons in his life; he does so in the manner of sending out a trial balloon—to test the reaction of the caseworker. If the caseworker accepts this revelation, not in a manner of approving or disapproving but as a part of reality, the client ceases to need a defense for that particular item. The client will continue to test out the worker until he senses that the caseworker accepts him as he is, with his strengths and weaknesses, his successes and failures, without approving or disapproving and without making the client feel less a person. As this continues, the client loses his need for the defenses, which he recognizes as unproductive and undesirable, and feels a sense of safety, sensing that whatever he says is understood by the caseworker and is used to help him. As he grows in comfortableness in revealing himself, he begins to be able to face himself as he is, to explore the negatives, and to dispose himself toward· helping himself more effectively. As the caseworker accepts him, the client begins to accept himself. He does not feel that the caseworker is a threat to him; he begins to be himself, thus developing his greatest strength. He may be only vaguely aware of this process, and will verbalize what is happening by a simple expression such as, "I never was able to talk to anyone like this before."

The client's change in regard to himself, by accepting himself, gives a new and unique character to his efforts to help himself. Possibly for the first time in his life his feelings and attitudes are recognized as real and significant, because for the first time he is met with no approval or disapproval. An inner change takes place that furnishes a basis for confidence, which will prevent the client from yielding to fears and resentments that arise naturally out of his uncomfortable situation.

THE ROLE OF THE CASEWORKER

Conscious of his role as a professional helping person, the caseworker realizes the importance of keeping the casework relationship on a realistic basis. He is in constant search for pertinent reality. He wants to see not only the client's strengths and successes; he also wants to see the client's weaknesses and failures, insofar as they pertain to the purpose of this particular case. The first step in doing something about a problem is to recognize it. Therefore the caseworker desires to see the reality regardless of its unpleasantness, to perceive it when it is revealed, and to strive to understand what it means to the client and his problem. Moreover, the caseworker does not merely wait passively for this revelation, but actively stimulates such revelations, on the basis of sound diagnostic clues and at the pace of the client.

When the client expresses negative feelings or attitudes about himself, about the people in his life, or even about the caseworker, the caseworker welcomes these expressions and is happy that the client was able to express them. The caseworker is not happy that the client *has* these negative feelings, but rather that he *was able to express* them, because thereby a real and pertinent part of the client's problem which was hidden became known, thus making treatment possible.

Although comparisons are always imperfect, the caseworker's acceptance of negatives in the client is somewhat similar to the physician's acceptance of a patient's symptoms. The doctor seeks and welcomes the revelations of the symptoms in order to make an accurate diagnosis. If the patient complains of a shortage of breath, the doctor wants to know if this indicates pathology in the heart, the lungs, or the stomach. He welcomes pertinent information and is glad when all the facts are revealed. He is not happy that the patient is ill, but rather he is happy that he identified correctly the nature of the illness. Identification of the difficulty is the first step in doing something about it. The principal difference in this comparison is that the medical patient is more passive than the casework client; seeing the reality is important both to the caseworker and the client because the client is the principal agent in the casework helping process. Acceptance of the client is necessary in every phase of the processes of study, diagnosis, and treatment.

It is the client who initiates the establishment of the casework relationship by his coming to the agency, but the degree of ease with which he is able to follow through depends largely on whether the attitude of the caseworker permits him to express himself. The fact of his coming calls for a definite response from the worker.

> The client comes because he has problems he cannot solve, he is frustrated, he seeks advice or assistance. . . . His coming is the result of a certain amount of cogitation and he is ready to tell his story—always, no doubt, with a certain amount of bias. He is ready to go through with a new experience. He is led in this by the case worker. Her mood is receptive, without prejudice. His is one of outpouring. . . . His freedom of expression should be encouraged, his thoughts and plans should be heeded. He should be drawn out with the idea of having him see his own problems in the light of day and therefore better understand himself.[17]

The first characteristic of this response is that it is client-focused, directed to the needs of the client rather than to the worker's own needs.

> Social case work differs from the ordinary relationships in social life in one important respect. It is oriented one way—toward the client's need. The professional worker does not expect to get

from the client, as he could rightly expect to get from his friends, sympathy or advice, nor does he ask the client to serve his interests.[18]

The caseworker will be of little use to clients unless he has a real interest in them—cares about them—but he can never be helpful if he exploits this interest in the form of curiosity or a desire to manage, or a need to have clients love him for what he does for them.[19]

The second characteristic is that the caseworker realizes the potential of the client for self-help and exercises professional responsibility for the promotion of the growth of the client.

The worker must be one who likes, understands, and is able to be tolerant of human emotions of every kind, but who can at the same time expect the best from an individual, and often insist that he carry out this best.[20]

One knows that growth depends first of all on securing the means of subsistence, then on opportunity, but finally on facing immediate reality, accepting responsibility, and working not only against limitations but also with and within them.[21]

The client should face his problem as his own. He should not be allowed to unload his problem on the worker; only his feeling about the problem should be accepted. In this way he is kept better able to meet his own situations later on.[22]

The third characteristic of the response is that it contains both thought and feeling elements. On the thought level it implies a clear awareness of purpose and a knowledge of human personality and patterns of behavior.

The greatest gift is to enable another to realize his own capacities for change and growth. One cannot, however, release such energies in a client unless the helper himself has been taught systematically to understand the nature of motivation—how a person feels about his situation, about others, about the worker as "counselor" or "therapist." Only if the social worker in his professional education has been well grounded psychologically can he help the client to mobilize his feelings in the direction of change, growth, and adaptation to reality.[23]

On the emotional level acceptance of the client necessarily involves the use of self in the relationship. And the use of self professionally, with a purpose, can be achieved only through a knowledge of self.

This knowledge of self is acquired through observation and practice. It calls for a willingness on the part of the worker to observe his own behavior in operation and to evaluate it in the light of professional understanding and responsibility.

> The worker, as part of his acquisition of knowledge and skill, must to a considerable degree become willing to see himself in operation and observe how his acts affect others in his professional operations. In other words, if he is to use the self in his social skills in casework . . . he must understand the dynamics of self. He grows conscious of his role in all sorts of situations.[24]

> During the field-training experience the student is helped to notice and to respond to feelings in clients, and by discussing his own mistakes, analyzing his reactions both to client and to supervisor, he gradually becomes aware of the meaning of interaction. Thus, he begins at one and the same time, as he lays aside his defenses against seeing his own patterns of behavior, to achieve a greater objectivity and control.[25]

Self-awareness leads to the acceptance of self and ultimately to the acceptance of others. The perception of one's own attitudes and feelings and responses to problems helps one to accept another person's attitudes, feelings, and responses to difficulty. It is the caseworker's understanding of these as he has experienced them in himself that enables the worker to understand these feelings and attitudes in others. This does not mean, however, that the caseworker must have experienced the same problems as the client in order to be helpful; but the caseworker in his life's experience has had problems of some variety. How he reacted to these problems will have some similarity to the way the client reacts to his.

The fourth characteristic of the response to the client is that it receives direction from the function of the agency. The service which the agency offers to its clients influences the worker's acceptance of the client. It specifies the conditions under which the person with the problem is accepted. Since acceptance means perceiving and dealing with the client as he is, the extent to which the client is helped to reveal himself is determined by the service offered by the agency. Disproportionate study and diagnosis are thus avoided, as well as treatment plans which the agency is unable to implement.

OBSTACLES TO ACCEPTANCE

The potential impediments to the caseworker's acceptance of the client are many. Most impediments stem, however, from one source: the caseworker's lack of self-awareness in some area. This impedes the caseworker from perceiving pertinent reality and from dealing with the client as he really is.

Before enumerating particular impediments to acceptance, a general observation seems indicated. Acceptance is not an all-or-nothing phenomenon, like perfect sight or total blindness. Rather, every caseworker has a certain degree of skill in acceptance, and this degree may vary from day to day or from client to client. No caseworker has, or is expected to have, perfect acceptance, for that would require a godlike wisdom and an immunity from human frailties. In the practice of every caseworker, however, there is always room for improvement, and there is a professional obligation to strive continually toward greater skill in the acceptance of the people we serve.

The following enumeration of obstacles to acceptance is meant to be illustrative rather than exhaustive:

1. *Insufficient knowledge of patterns of human behavior*. The caseworker needs psychological and psychiatric knowledge, especially concerning the patterns of human behavior in times of stress, the common emotional reactions to social and economic problems, and the ordinary defense mechanisms. This knowledge serves as a framework for the understanding of individuals and, in specific reference to acceptance, it sharpens the eyes of the caseworker to see pertinent reality factors in each client's case. Without such a framework the caseworker does not know what to look for, and therefore will miss much that is real and pertinent.

2. *Nonacceptance of something in self*. It is possible that the caseworker perceives, in some degree, negative and undesirable factors in the client's situation which are quite similar to something in the caseworker's. This may be almost anything. It may be a dislike for a mother-in-law, a fear of economic insecurity, or an ambivalence about one's own children. If the caseworker suppresses these unresolved conflicts in himself, he will find it difficult to help the client face them when it is good casework to do so. Because the caseworker could not deal with these realistically in his own life, he will be unable to deal with them as realities in the client's life.

> . . . one of the essentials of treating others is understanding and facing ourselves. The social worker is, of course, not free from unlovely motives, but he will not prove really helpful to others unless he has learned to recognize these bad as well as good impulses in himself—learned to accept them as fact—and in spite of them, developed his capacity to "love" many different kinds of persons, or at least keep from injuring them by being aware of the less admirable feelings that persist within.[26]

3. *Imputing to the client one's own feelings*. Self-awareness means, among other things, an awareness of one's own attitudes

and feelings. This helps the caseworker to see himself as an individual, with individual reactions and differences. Without this awareness the caseworker is liable to follow his natural tendency to impute his own feelings to the client. He is apt to cut off the client's expression of his feelings, mistakenly concluding that he knows what the client's feelings about a particular situation are. Thus he actually does not perceive reality as it is. As a consequence he does not deal with the client as he really is. The client will vaguely feel this as a very subtle form of rejection.

4. *Biases and prejudices.* It is hoped that the professional social worker has a conscious awareness of tendencies to the gross biases and prejudices arising from differences in race, creed, culture, and economic status. Tendencies to more subtle biases, however, are more difficult to detect in oneself. A pessimism about the rehabilitative possibilities of parolees who are above a certain age is a bias which can impede acceptance. A conviction that the basic problem of all unmarried mothers is a poor relationship of the girl with her mother can blind the caseworker to other basic causes. A conviction that adoption is the best plan for all children born out of wedlock can prevent the caseworker, in some instances, from dealing with the full reality in the case.

5. *Unwarranted reassurances.* The caseworker's reassurance of a client, in some instances, can be a form of psychological support; it is also a method of helping the client postpone temporarily the facing of a difficult reality, when it is clear that he is not strong enough to face it at the time. Reassurances, however, can be unwarranted; they are then equivalently a refusal on the part of the caseworker to deal with reality. In a case of marital counseling, for example, the wife raised the discussion that her husband's excessive drinking might be due to some fault in herself. Instead of pursuing this line of thought and exploring the wife's feelings in the matter, the caseworker said that the wife need not blame herself; that the drinking was partly rooted in her husband's personality and partly an escape from worry caused by his

business responsibilities.[27] Clearly, this reassurance prevented the client from bringing into the open her own feelings. The caseworker, in effect, refused to accept something which in all probability was pertinent to the case.

6. *Confusion between acceptance and approval.* The social worker, as every adult, has a philosophy of life which includes convictions about moral right and wrong in human behavior. It also includes opinions about what is socially desirable or undesirable, acceptable or unacceptable. In his own personal life these standards are indispensable guides in living. Actually, the profession needs to recognize more deeply than it currently does the existence of objective standards of human behavior and to incorporate them into the philosophy of the profession. Subjective opinions, individual interpretations, and personal tastes are legitimate in some things; but unless a few things are considered sacred, unchangeable, and permanent, life ceases to have meaning and personal integrity is impossible. The individual social worker and the profession as a whole need to be clear about what they approve and disapprove. Social workers, in order to be effective in helping people, must ally themselves with the civil law, with the moral law, and with social and economic standards which promote decency and dignity in human affairs. Clarity in this area contributes to professional maturity.

The role of the caseworker is to help the client proceed from a situation which is undesirable and unacceptable to a situation which is desirable and acceptable. Therefore some standard of right and wrong, of good and bad, is implicit in every case. The violation of the moral law by the unmarried mother, the violation of civil law by the parolee, the emotional rejection of her child by a mother seeking help in a child-guidance clinic, the breakup of a family through divorce, the fears which prevent the person from employment—all of these are undesirable. It is therefore ridiculous to think that the caseworker's duty is to approve of everything about the client. The client comes for help because he is unhappy about something in his life; he does not approve of everything in himself.

The caseworker must nevertheless accept the client and everything about the client that is pertinent to the helping process. The caseworker must accept even those elements of which he disapproves. He accepts the unmarried mother's verbalization about her ambivalence about sexual behavior, in the technical sense of acceptance, which means that her ambivalence is real, is pertinent to her problem, and is discussed with a therapeutic purpose. He accepts the parolee's negative attitudes to law, to law-enforcement officers, to his past imprisonment, and to the parole regulations. Even though the caseworker is duty-bound to be allied with the law, he accepts the parolee's attitudes because they are a part of the problem and need to be aired out, clarified, and straightened out. He accepts the verbal protestations of the rejecting mother to the effect that she is a good mother and not at all responsible for her child's problems, because she needs help in gaining insight into her unsatisfactory relationship with her child.

Acceptance, therefore, is a technical term. The object of acceptance is reality; the caseworker perceives and deals with the client as he is in reality. The client's congenial and uncongenial qualities, his positive and negative feelings, his acceptable and unacceptable attitudes and behavior, need to be perceived and dealt with both by the client and the caseworker. Otherwise, casework becomes an unreal, make-believe situation. As the physician accepts every pertinent bit of information about the patient's physical health, the caseworker in like manner accepts everything pertinent about the client's psychosocial health.

7. *Loss of respect for the client.* In the process of revealing his weaknesses and failures and in facing them realistically there is a possibility that the client will think less of himself and lose his sense of personal dignity and worth. The possibility will become a reality if the caseworker begins to lose respect for the client; if he does, he will be unable to hide it from the client.

Acceptance is based upon a philosophical conviction that a person has an innate dignity and worth which is derived from his filial relationship to God and which cannot be lost by the individual's weakness and failure. However, the consciousness and the feeling of one's worth can be lost. It is possible that the client can lose this consciousness and feeling of personal dignity and value if the caseworker loses respect for the client.

Acceptance requires one of the qualities of love. In real love, of whatever variety, the two persons know each other; they know their weaknesses and strengths, their successes and failures, and in spite of them, possibly even because of them, mutual respect continues and even increases. Love and acceptance cease with a loss of respect. Respect for another person, necessarily implying a recognition of his innate dignity and value, is an internal attitude. This internal attitude is expected of a professional helping person, and is the result of his self-awareness and his philosophy of life.

8. *Overidentification.* Acceptance and a good relationship imply an internal emotional response from the caseworker, therapeutically directed to the client's problem. This response produces a professional identification of the caseworker with the client. Identification is a necessary ingredient in effective helping. Identification, as every other element in the relationship, has degrees. And, as every other good thing, it can be overdone, at which point it ceases to be a good.

The root of overidentification is, again, a lack of self-awareness on the part of the caseworker. Recognizing something in the client which is very akin to something in his own life, the caseworker emotionally responds in a way which meets his own needs rather than the client's. It may be such an intense concern about some area of the client's situation that the caseworker assumes the principal responsibility for it. It may be the recognition of injustice done to the client by some person or some circumstance, but it is felt by the caseworker in such an extreme way that he unconsciously feels that he himself was the victim of the injustice.

It may be taking sides with the child against the parent, the wife against the husband, the client against the agency. It may be the caseworker's striving to gratify his own need for affection through the client. Thus the caseworker ceases to be a professional helping person to the degree of his overidentification, because he has confused his own problems and needs with those of the client.

Overidentification with the client, from whatever motive, creates a blind spot in the caseworker, impeding the perception of things as they really are and therefore endangering the effectiveness of the total helping process.

The client responds in two ways to the accepting attitude of the worker. In relation to himself, he becomes freer from tension and anxiety which arise from the fear of rejection. He finds it less necessary as the relationship progresses to protect himself from acknowledging his deeper feelings and attitudes, and the value they have for him. Though this in itself will not remove his difficulties, the growing recognition of his inner and most protected feelings about himself and others may help him to face his difficulty constructively.

In his relationship with the worker, acceptance frees the client to engage himself in this specific relationship, to express what he really thinks and feels without thought of what the worker would want to hear. It provides the basis for an ongoing relationship, and the security it provides may compensate for the anxiety produced by temporary disturbances within the client as he gives information about himself and his problem to the caseworker. The acceptance which the client perceives permits him to reveal himself with his limitations and mistakes, without detriment to his inner sense of dignity.

ENDNOTES FOR PRINCIPLE 4

1 *Social Case Work: Generic and Specific*, p. 11.
2 "Social Work Semantics." *Journal of Social Casework* 30:340, October 1949.
3 Bertha Capen Reynolds, "A Changing Psychology in Social Case Work—After One Year." *The Family* 13:107, June 1932.

4 Florence Hollis, *Women in Marital Conflict*, p. 197 note. New York: Family Service Association of America, 1949.

5 Hertha Kraus, "The Role of Social Casework in American Social Work." *Social Casework* 31:9, January 1950.

6 Hamilton, *Theory and Practice of Social Case Work*, p. 52.

7 Joseph Nuttin, *Psychoanalysis and Personality*, translated by George Lamb, pp. 98-99. New York: Sheed and Ward, 1953.

8 Mary J. McCormick, *Diagnostic Casework in the Thomistic Pattern*, p. 105. New York: Columbia University Press, 1954.

9 Swithun Bowers, O.M.I., "Social Work and Human Problems." *Social Casework* 35:190, May 1954.

10 Hamilton, *Theory and Practice of Social Case Work*, p. 40.

11 Department of the Army, *Military Psychiatric Social Work*, p. 13.

12 Herbert Hewitt Stroup, *Social Work, An Introduction to the Field*, p. 28. New York: American Book Company, 1948.

13 Charles R. McKenney, S.J., *Moral Problems in Social Work*, p. 59. Milwaukee: Bruce Publishing Company, 1951.

14 Russell W. Davenport, *The Dignity of Man*, pp. 231-32. New York: Harper and Brothers, 1955.

15 Edward P. Cronan, *The Dignity of the Human Person*, p. 124. New York: Philosophical Library, 1955.

16 *Ibid.*, p. 203.

17 Mary Arden Young, "Supervision—A Worm's Eye View." *The Family* 11:45, April 1930.

18 Bertha Capen Reynolds, "Social Case Work: What Is It? What Is Its Place in the World Today?" *The Family* 16:240, December 1935.

19 Hamilton, *Theory and Practice of Social Case Work*, pp. 40-41.

20 O. Spurgeon English, "The Significance of Social Case Work." *The Family* 20:179, October 1939.

21 Hamilton, *Theory and Practice of Social Case Work*, p. 10.

22 Helen M. Walker, "The Aide in Action." *The Family* 14:299, December 1933.

23 Hamilton, *Theory and Practice of Social Case Work*, pp. 22-23.

24 *Ibid.*, p. 43.

25 *Ibid.*

26 Hamilton, "Helping People—The Growth of a Profession," p. 296.

27 Hollis, *Women in Marital Conflict*, pp. 179-80.

Principle 5

THE NONJUDGMENTAL ATTITUDE

THE HEBREWS in the Old Testament and the Christians in the New Testament are taught not to judge their fellow man: "Do you accept his person, and do you endeavor to judge for God?" (Job 13:8); "Do not judge, that you may not be judged" (Matthew 7:1); "Therefore let us no longer judge one another" (Romans 14:13); "But thou who judgest thy neighbor, who art thou?" (James 4:13).

Psychiatry and social work have recognized the wisdom of this admonition and have adopted it as a principle of action in helping troubled people. Unfortunately, in some schools of psychiatry the adoption of this principle has contributed to a denial of an objective standard of right and wrong in human affairs. The nonjudgmental attitude in social work is not only compatible with objective norms in human behavior but actually requires them. The attitude can be defined as follows:

> **The nonjudgmental attitude is a quality of the casework relationship; it is based on a conviction that the casework function excludes assigning guilt or innocence, or degree of client responsibility for causation of the problems or needs, but does include making evaluative judgments about the attitudes, standards, or actions of the client; the attitude, which involves both thought and feeling elements, is transmitted to the client.**

The fundamental meaning of "judging" is to determine whether a person is innocent or guilty of doing wrong. It is the process of deciding whether or not a person committed an evil act with knowledge and intent and, therefore, is blamable for it.

In casework, judging would mean an attempt to place blame upon the client, declaring him, either verbally or nonverbally, responsible for causing his problems or his dependency, whether they are environmental or in his personality. For example, it would mean that the caseworker would decide the guilt or innocence of the applicant for old-age assistance as a lifelong spendthrift; of the unmarried mother as a violator of the sixth commandment; of the parolee as a violator of a civil law; of the rejecting mother as a selfish woman; of the relatives of a patient in a mental hospital as contributors to his illness; of parents placing their children in a foster home as parental failures.

In helping clients it is important to understand their failures and weaknesses, but it is not the function of the caseworker to judge. The right and the power to make judgments are vested in certain authorities. Judgments by persons without authority constitute a violation of a basic human right. In some settings certain authoritative powers may be inherent in the agency's function, but even there the authority vested in the social worker is merely the equivalent of a police power. In no setting does he have judicial authority, either legal or moral.

The philosophy of social work has grown in love and optimism by recognizing that judgments of the person are irrelevant, unmerciful, and hazardous. At an early period in social work the client's "worthiness" or "unworthiness" was a consideration in giving or withholding help. The degree of the client's guilt or innocence in creating his difficulty was a point that had to be established; if he was found guilty, he often was not helped. This criterion in social work was based on the false assumption that the individual would inevitably repeat his unacceptable behavior if he did not suffer for his past misdeeds; that human failure was always due to a perverse will and a coldly deliberate evil act. Today social work accepts the Christian concept that it is possible to love the sinner without loving his sin. Need rather than "worthiness" has come to be accepted as the criterion for eligibility for service, in both public and private agencies. Social work also recognizes the therapeutic principle that antipathy and hate vitiate the potentials of the helping relationship; the theory that one may hate the sinner along with the sin is not tenable. Aid rather than punishment is the function of social work.

In order to help the client mobilize the resources of the community and his own inner capacities toward the solution of his problems, toward a better adjustment, and toward a strength and a growth of his personality, the caseworker has to understand the client in a degree proportionate to his need or problem. In order to help effectively the caseworker must understand the causes of the client's problems. In this process, however, there is no reason to judge the guilt or innocence of the client or to assign blame to him or to others for the causation of his problem.

THE NEED OF THE CLIENT

When a person comes to a social agency for help, he has a feeling of inadequacy, of weakness, and possibly of failure. The intensity of this feeling will vary with clients. Coming to a social agency means that the client is incapable of coping alone with some area of his life. The necessity of seeking help from an agency can produce a host of painful feelings.

One of the feelings is a fear of being judged. The basis for the fear is that in his previous life experiences he has been judged and condemned for his mistakes and failures by people who neither understood him nor had a right to pass sentence upon him. He sees the caseworker as the symbol of a society whose critical judgment he fears. He is afraid of being labeled a failure, an inadequate person, or a moral weakling. As a result the client tends to seek safety in a self-protective attitude, thereby constructing an obstacle to looking objectively at himself and at the causes of his maladjustment.

Both the verbalized and the nonverbalized passing of judgment upon the person are beyond the function of the caseworker. The client, because of his emotional sensitivity and guilt feelings, will inevitably feel the nonverbalized judgmental attitude. It is something that cannot be hidden from him; if the caseworker has it, even though it is unspoken, it will be felt by the client.

As long as the client fears judgment, he will not feel free to talk about himself with ease and openness. He will not be able to reveal the negatives in his situation and in his personality, which are pertinent to his case, because he fears that the information may be used against him in some way. He will be excessively sensitive to criticism, uneasy about the possible reaction of the caseworker, and uncertain about what it is safe to reveal and what it is wise to hide.[1]

The client is similarly affected by the more subtle form of judgment, namely, by praise and approval. He may develop the feeling that the worker accepts him conditionally and that he is fortunate to have been judged favorably. He may feel compelled to remain within the good graces of the caseworker by presenting himself only in a favorable light. Blame and praise may have an identical effect upon the client: to urge him to hide a part of himself.

The need for self-protection gradually diminishes as the client slowly recognizes the caseworker as a person who is totally disinterested in condemning or praising him.[2] His suspiciousness of the friendliness of the caseworker is allayed and he becomes convinced that questions are asked in order to help rather than to harm him. Assured of the caseworker's nonjudgmental attitude, he grows in the ability to express himself without fear of condemnation. He becomes more able to accept himself as a person of worth and consequently more able to discuss his real needs and problems. Breathing the invigorating air of the nonjudgmental atmosphere created by the caseworker, the client develops strength to look at himself objectively, to reveal himself in the interviews as he really is and as he sees himself, and to do what is necessary for constructive change.

VALUES AND STANDARDS NECESSARY

To confuse the nonjudgmental attitude with indifference to social, legal, and moral standards would be tragic. The nonjudgmental attitude does not mean indifference to or rejection of value systems.

This is the key distinction: the caseworker prescinds from judging the guilt or innocence of the *client;* but the caseworker objectively evaluates the *attitudes, standards, and actions* of the client. The client feels hurt when *he* is judged; he is not necessarily hurt if his *behavior* is evaluated. The caseworker's motive and purpose in evaluating the behavior of the client is clear: to understand rather than to judge the client. The caseworker has an interest in the deviation from standards and values, but not for the purpose of assigning blame. He is interested in the causes of the client's behavior only insofar as this understanding is an aid in furthering the client's present and future adjustment. For a sound diagnostic evaluation he needs to know the client's ego strengths and weaknesses, and his conflicts toward a healthy adjustment to reality.

Standards and values, being a part of reality, are not only compatible with the nonjudgmental attitude, but are indispensable for effective casework help. Three reasons are offered in confirmation of this conviction.

First, the caseworker, because he is a social worker, has a *social* responsibility; he is an agent, a representative, of the community, whether employed in a public or a private agency. By profession he is necessarily allied with social, legal, and moral good. His function is to help the individual within the law and within the basic values of a society which is based upon the belief in God.

Second, the client will not be helped if he finds that the caseworker is indifferent to the antisocial, illegal, or immoral attitudes or standards that brought trouble to the client. To an unmarried mother, for example, who feels and verbalizes guilt, a remark such as "Marriage, after all, is only a social convention," is unrealistic and futile, and may harm the client. It is unrealistic because the client lives in a society where marriage standards are real and definite. It is futile because the denial of the reality situation will not remove her guilt feelings. It may also be harmful; the client usually would reject the variant standard implicit in such a statement and would feel that the caseworker does not understand her problem and, therefore, is incapable of helping. If the client should accept the full implication of the caseworker's remark, recidivism might result. Helping clients achieve standards is implicit in protective casework with such groups as probationers, parolees, and sex delinquents; it is also a particular goal in a number of other settings.

Third, to maintain the integrity of his own personality the caseworker cannot remain interiorly indifferent to standards contrary to his own. If, for example, a client were engaged in behavior which the caseworker considers contrary to the natural law binding all people, the caseworker could not be expected to change his own philosophy with each case. He must remain true to himself. He has a right to his own sense of social, moral, and spiritual values, personally and professionally.[3] However, this does not necessarily mean that the caseworker will be moralistic with the client, or that he will impose his own personal code of ethics upon the client. He knows that every man has a right to follow his own conscience; this principle will be applicable in many cases. In some instances, however, where subjectivity of interpretation would result in antisocial or illegal behavior, the limitations to client self-determination would be recognized and applied in the casework way.

Does the caseworker ever need to verbalize his evaluation of the client's unacceptable behavior or standards? It depends upon the functioning of the personality. If the client's acceptance of healthy standards of behavior is unimpaired, even though conflict exists, the evaluation may not need to be verbalized, because the client usually is able to make such appraisals himself in the security of a good relationship. If, however, the client has begun to reject objectively healthy standards of behavior in his effort to ease the tensions in his life, verbalized evaluations may be indicated. When based on adequate diagnosis and a strong relationship, comments and interpretations about deviant behavior are appropriate and often necessary techniques.

In this difficult matter the nature of the standard or value needs to be clearly understood. There are basic, vital values at one end of the scale and relatively unimportant ones at the other end, with many degrees in between. There are important values such as legal conformance and morality, and relatively unimportant ones such as standards of housekeeping, about which there may be legitimate personal difference of opinion and taste.

THE EMOTIONAL COMPONENT

The nonjudgmental attitude is an unverbalized inner conviction, based upon the awareness that judging the client as a person is contrary to a basic right and therapeutically harmful. This conviction, in order to be a dynamic force in the relationship, must contain both thought and feeling elements. It cannot remain on a purely intellectual level.

The reason for this is rather elemental: the client needs to be met at the level of his problem. And the client's fear of being judged is both on the thought and feeling levels. Because of the nature of human beings the fear is not always a rational one. The caseworker, therefore, needs to be sensitive to the client's feelings about his shortcomings, whether real or imaginary, and must be able to respond on the feeling level. A response on a purely thought level is inadequate. We speak of the caseworker's controlled emotional involvement as one of the components of the casework relationship. If the caseworker accepts the nonjudgmental attitude only on an intellectual level, he will not be able to transmit adequate assurance to the client; he will not be sensitive to the client's feelings in this area nor be able to respond to them in a helping way. To be effective the nonjudgmental attitude of the caseworker must be felt by the client; and the client will feel it only if the caseworker feels it.

How does the caseworker get to feel it? An adequate answer to this question would involve a discussion of the entire casework relationship, and understandably so, because the nonjudgmental attitude is only conceptually separable from the relationship as a whole. However, two areas can be indicated as specifically pertinent: the caseworker's self-awareness and his sensitivity to the client's feeling about being judged.

Self-awareness is frequently understood only in a very limited sense: an awareness of undesirable things in oneself, of things to be eliminated or modified in oneself. However, it can also be the source of positive learning about human nature and behavior. Academic instruction, reading, and supervised practice are the principal sources of learning the dynamics of human behavior, but these can be enriched at times by a more intimate knowledge which comes from introspection, by learning how one's own self operates. A consciously developed awareness of how he feels when other people judge him will help the caseworker understand in a more complete way how the client feels about being judged. A reflection upon his own life's experiences and upon his own interpersonal relationships will help to formulate a conviction about judging which will contain emotional elements. Actually, all knowledge of the dynamics of human nature will remain purely intellectual, academic, static, and doubtfully useful in casework unless it is confirmed and tested, consciously or otherwise, through a healthy introspection. The caseworker, after all, is a human being, the object of his professional study, and he has essentially the same human nature as his clients.

To feel the nonjudgmental attitude the caseworker needs to be sensitive to the client's feelings, and specifically to his feelings about being judged and about guilt resulting from dependence, defeat, and failure. Since the client's problem is psychosocial even when his expressed request is for tangible material goods, he has uncomfortable feelings about seeking help. These feelings may be more intense and possibly more hidden at the beginning, but we can validly assume that they are present in some degree most of the time. They may or may not be verbalized by the client, but they can be seen by the sensitive caseworker in the tone of the client's speech, in what he does not say, in his silences, in his face and eyes, in his posture, in the use of his hands, and in his total bearing. All these can tell, even more accurately than words, about the feelings. As the caseworker sees them and understands their meaning, he will be helped to respond on the feeling level.

TRANSMITTED TO THE CLIENT

The caseworker's nonjudgmental attitude needs to be felt by the client. However, there are no tricks, magical formulas, or pat phrases for transmitting an attitude; there are no set verbalized responses. It is conveyed to the client primarily in the tone and manner of interviewing, rather than in direct statements such as, "I am not judging you, but trying to learn about you and your problem in order to be helpful." Verbalizing this attitude may be helpful in some cases, but only if it complements the internal feeling. No words can effectively convey a nonjudgmental attitude if the caseworker does not possess it interiorly.

The first interviews are especially important; the client should be helped to feel secure enough to talk easily about his problem so that a sound basis for joint planning can be established. When the client feels that he is free to tell his story in his own way and when he gets the caseworker's full attention, he senses that his relationship with the caseworker is different from his relationships with other people who had little respect for him. This does not mean that the caseworker's nonjudgmental attitude is established at a given point of time and can then be taken for granted; it is an ongoing, essential quality throughout all stages of the relationship, growing and deepening along with the relationship.

Prejudices can be an obstacle to the caseworker's having and transmitting the nonjudgmental attitude. The caseworker, like every human being, probably has to a greater or lesser degree some prejudices and biases. He may have conscious or unconscious dislikes of some personality types. It is difficult to be nonjudgmental about persons whom we naturally dislike or against whom we are prejudiced. "Liking" a client may not always be necessary for effective casework, but striving to be free from prejudice is. The caseworker, therefore, needs to recognize and control these biases within himself and to develop his capacity to see people objectively, as they are, rather than subjectively, as they appear through the colored glass of his own prejudices.

A premature assurance that the client's problem is understood, aside from being wrong in all probability and discouraging the client from talking about it, can give the client the impression that the caseworker is a person who jumps at conclusions and is liable to be judgmental about him. The client knows that he has not told the whole story and he may be hesitant to do so to a caseworker who is in a hurry.

A reference to other people with similar problems, either for the purpose of comparison or illustration, gives the client the impression that the caseworker is putting the client into a category. Clients are usually disinterested in comparisons and they resent classifications because they represent types of judgment.

Another obstacle to maintaining a nonjudgmental attitude is the client's expression of negative feelings, such as hostility, to the caseworker. Frequently this is a displacement of feelings, a transference of feelings that the client originally had to other persons in his life. Unless the caseworker is aware of these defense mechanisms and understands their meaning, the attitude may be difficult to maintain. As the caseworker grows in the awareness that these feelings are helpful in understanding the client, he feels less threatened personally, more secure in his professional role, and finds the nonjudgmental attitude somewhat easier to maintain and transmit.

ENDNOTES FOR PRINCIPLE 5

1 Stroup, *Social Work, An Introduction to the Field*, pp. 90-91.
2 Hamilton, *Theory and Practice of Social Case Work*, p. 40.
3 Department of the Army, *Military Psychiatric Social Work*, p. 13; McKenney, *Moral Problems in Social Work*, pp. 56-59; Hamilton, "Helping People —The Growth of a Profession," p. 297.

Principle 6

CLIENT SELF-DETERMINATION

CASEWORKERS are not philosophers by profession and seem to have little inclination in that direction. However, since they enter people's lives in a very practical and intimate way, they necessarily become involved in issues which have an inescapable connection with the philosophy of human living.

Social workers are precipitated into philosophical considerations that take on practical importance when we consider of what it is that our practice consists. Questions about the nature of the self and other selves, the nature of reality, of consciousness, of determinism, of science, of reason, and of the function of the will cannot be evaded, because we are technicians who work with people and people live in a social world, in a world of change, of continuity, and of habit.[1]

Today one of the firmest convictions of the profession of social work is that the person has an innate ability for self-determination and that a conscious, willful violation of the client's freedom by a caseworker is an unprofessional act which transgresses the client's natural right and impairs casework treatment or makes it impossible. This conviction slowly developed over a period of more than thirty years.

By 1920 the casework profession had long since renounced the attitude of the English poor laws toward the client. However dependent he may have been, he was recognized as a human being with certain God-given and inalienable rights to live his own life.

From 1920 to 1930 there was a growing awareness that the client had a right and a need to participate actively in the decisions and choices in the casework process. This awareness was born of the belief that all men are free agents by nature; it was nurtured by the concept of democratic living; and it was confirmed by the pragmatic observation that casework treatment was truly effective only when the client made his own choices and decisions. The cultural residue of the old attitudes to the client, however, did not disappear completely. The "participation" of the client in treatment plans was the expression of the highest ideal regarding client freedom in this era. Not all caseworkers subscribed to this ideal. Others professed it, but for various reasons found it difficult or impossible to apply in practice. The socioeconomic conditions, especially the large number of illiterate immigrants, the economic depression of the early thirties, and the general public's lack of understanding of the casework process complicated the application of the democratic ideal. Client participation made the casework process slower, while the condition of the times called for speed. Also, since the ideal was comparatively new in welfare work, the realistic modifications of client freedom had not yet been worked out on a practical level by overburdened supervisors and caseworkers.

From 1930 to 1940 the concept of client freedom was slowly purified and many of the practical problems arising from it were clarified. The right of the client was seen as extending beyond mere "participation"; such phrases as "self-help" and "making his own plans and decisions" indicated that the chief responsibility for plan making was shifted from the caseworker to the client. In this era a number of trends in casework aided the growth and development of client freedom. The emphasis in casework changed from diagnosis to treatment, and the client's ability to make his own choices and formulate his own plans were considered both a means and a goal of treatment, an aid to personality maturity and a test of it. The vigorous new interest in the casework relationship contributed to the advancement of client self-determination, because the latter was considered an essential ingredient of the former. Finally the advent of new types of clients, including indigents during the great depression who came from the same social and economic strata as the caseworker and other clients who could pay for casework services, emphasized as never before the necessity and practicality of client self-determination.

The interest in client freedom at this time manifested itself less in connection with the theory and more in connection with the practical aspects. The function of the caseworker in reference to client freedom was more concretely detailed. Perhaps the greatest contribution was the balancing of the ideal with the realities of the casework situation. The principle of self-determination, it was now recognized, had to be individuated to the ability of clients; not all clients were equally capable of making their own decisions. The limitations to client freedom arising from civil and moral law, and from the function of the agency, were discussed at considerable length in casework literature. This was an era of self-criticism. Caseworkers copiously recorded in their literature the shortcomings and failures of practitioners in regard to client freedom. As in the previous decade, there was a gap between the ideal and the actual practice; but there were indications that the gap was not so large and that it was rapidly diminishing.

From 1940 to 1950 the trend to incorporate the ideal into daily practice continued. The literature of social work contained discussions of how caseworkers applied the ideal to a variety of casework settings, in public and private agencies, in authoritative and nonauthoritative agencies. The compatibility of the concept of authority with client self-determination was discussed at considerable length. Progress was made in spite of the fact that the casework profession, like the world at large, was undergoing many and serious disturbances. The war and its aftermath called for rapid readjustments in casework service. The influence of psychology and psychiatry, however, counterbalanced the disturbing elements and allowed the principle of client self-determination to maintain and even advance the status which it had won during the previous two decades. Currently, it is understood in the following terms:

> **The principle of client self-determination is the practical recognition of the right and need of clients to freedom in making their own choices and decisions in the casework process. Caseworkers have a corresponding duty to respect that right, recognize that need, stimulate and help to activate that potential for self-direction by helping the client to see and use the available and appropriate resources of the community and of his own personality. The client's right to self-determination, however, is limited by the client's capacity for positive and constructive decision making, by the framework of civil and moral law, and by the function of the agency.**

Throughout a thirty-year history the highest possible value has been placed upon the principle of client self-determination in casework; it would be difficult to imagine how its value could be assessed any higher. Client freedom was said to be (1) a necessary, fundamental right of the client flowing from his essential dignity as a human being; (2) a necessarily fundamental right of all individuals in a democratic society; (3) necessary for the effectiveness in casework service and treatment; and (4) an essential principle in casework philosophy. It is called a principle, a basic premise, a key concept, a foundation stone of social casework in all agencies and settings.

THE RIGHT AND THE NEED OF THE CLIENT

Like every human being, the client has the responsibility of living his life in such a manner as to achieve his life's goals, proximate and ultimate, as he conceives them. And since every responsibility is accompanied with corresponding rights, he is endowed by the Creator with a fundamental, inalienable right to choose and decide the appropriate means for the attaining of his own personal destiny.

As he receives the services of a social agency he has no intention, under ordinary circumstances, of surrendering either his basic right to freedom or any of its derivates. He comes to a social agency because he wants assistance with a need or problem. He believes that the social caseworker, because of his professional competence, can help him mobilize his own capacities and acquaint him with the resources in the community. He wants to know what choices are available to him and will welcome the caseworker's evaluation of each alternative. Although he may feel inadequate to meet his problems and although he may need the caseworker's psychological support in the process, he wants to remain free to make his own decisions.

The exercise of responsibility is one of the principal sources of personality growth and maturity. Only through the exercise of responsibility in free decisions can the client strive toward the maturity of his personality, intellectually, socially, emotionally, and spiritually. Specifically as a client, he needs freedom to make his own choices of the available means in order to make casework help effective. Social workers can give abundant testimony from long experience of the futility of casework when plans are superimposed upon the client. Social responsibility, emotional adjustment, and personality development are possible only when the person exercises his freedom of choice and decision.[2]

THE ROLE OF THE CASEWORKER

The caseworker is the person who is primarily responsible for applying the principle of client self-determination in practice. His understanding of his own role in the casework situation, and how he carries it out, manifest his attitude to client freedom. Presupposing that the client is capable of constructive self-determination and that he is contemplating decisions that are within the civil and the moral law and within the agency function, the caseworker's role can be stated positively and negatively. Positively, the following activities are considered to be in accord with the principle of client self-determination:

1. *To help the client see his problem or need clearly and with perspective.* The caseworker's diagnostic study and thinking, his acceptance of the client and identification with him, will help the client work through the emotional disturbance which the problem created and which deprived the client of clarity in seeing himself and his problem.[3]

2. *To acquaint the client with the pertinent resources in the community.* If there are alternatives in the available resources, the client is helped to see the significance of each choice. The caseworker expresses his own evaluation of each choice and offers suggestions, but in such a way that the client does not feel obliged to accept the caseworker's evaluation and follow his suggestions.

The role of the worker is a delicately balanced activity and passivity. The passivity consists of restraint in doing things for and to the client, thus helping the client to express himself as fully and as freely as he wishes. The remote activity consists in acquiring a knowledge of personality patterns which will be used in gaining an understanding of the particular personality of the client. The worker is active in observing and evaluating the words, actions, and emotions of the client, learning his strengths and weaknesses, enriching his inner and outer resources, and stimulating the client to his own activity.[4]

3. *To introduce stimuli that will activate the client's own dormant resources.* These stimuli consist in helping the client to free himself from fears and tensions, in giving him whatever support he may need, and in helping him grow through the interaction of personalities in the worker-client relationship.[5]

4. *To create a relationship environment in which the client can grow and work out his own problems.* The caseworker combines a listening, receptive attitude with active participation in which the client is helped to gain a deeper realization of his own person and his problems. The client, using his inner resources and the resources of the community, grows in the potential to work out his own problems, to move along at his own speed and in his own way.[6]

To summarize the role of the caseworker in a figure of speech, the caseworker opens doors and windows to let in air, light, and sunshine, so that the client can breathe more easily and see more clearly. The aim is to help him gain a better insight into his problem, and develop strength to help himself.[7]

Negatively, the following activities of a caseworker are considered to be at variance with the principle:

1. *To assume the principal responsibility for the working out of the problem and to allow the client to play only a subordinate role.* The extreme of this would be to determine the treatment plan and then superimpose it upon the client.

2. *To insist on a minute scrutiny of the social or emotional life of every client, regardless of the service he requests.* A disproportionate diagnosis, as some caseworkers have expressed it, reveals the total responsibility and the implied omniscience which

the caseworker is assuming. The supposition seems to be that, if the caseworker knows all, he can remedy all.[8]

3. *To manipulate, directly or indirectly.* By manipulation is meant the activity of maneuvering the client to choose or decide modes of action in accordance with the caseworker's judgment in such a way that the client is not aware of the process; or if he is aware of it, he feels "moved about" against his will.

4. *To persuade in a controlling way.* Such persuasion is understood to do more than put the client in possession of the facts to make his decision; it means to urge him to accept the caseworker's decision, in such a way as to weaken his freedom of choice and decision. This is equivalent to making the decisions and allowing the client the subordinate role of "participating" or "cooperating."

Summarizing the positive and negative activities, the principle of client self-determination does not narrow the scope of the caseworker's activity, except in the area of the client's choices and decisions. It encourages every other casework activity that can help the client help himself. The caseworker is urged to increase constantly his knowledge of personality structures which helps him to understand each client better. The caseworker is encouraged to develop skills in observing and understanding the meaning of the client's feelings and behavior in the interview sessions. In brief, the caseworker is very active in self-preparation for the role of a helping person, is zealous for the acquisition of the best thinking that is produced in casework and in the allied sciences, and develops proficiency in the best casework skills and techniques.

ILLUSTRATIONS

The following brief summaries illustrate the role of the caseworker in relatively uncomplicated cases. In each instance the client is free to choose from two or more alternatives.

Myrna, aged 17, raised from infancy in one foster home, under care of a private welfare agency, was found to be in need of vocational planning. Aptitude and psychological tests were administered to assist in the planning. The results indicated that Myrna had potentiality for general office work and for the operation of power sewing, and some ability in the field of commercial art. She was always considered by her very dominating foster mother to be a dull, physically weak child. Actually, she was neither: she scored in the average range in the Stanford-Binet Form L; a physical examination showed that she was healthy. Outwardly Myrna was docile, dependent, and had little initiative. She herself felt that she was "dumb." She expressed no particular preference about the types of employment suggested, nor about any other kind of job. The caseworker's function was to explore the advantages and disadvantages of the different available jobs, stimulate Myrna's interest, give her psychological support and encourage her in thinking independently, build up some confidence, and eventually select a job in which she would be comfortable.

Mrs. Allen, after a brief period of hospitalization, required several weeks of nursing care either in her own home or in a nursing home. The family agency was asked to help with the planning. There are three children, all of school age. The eldest, a high-school girl of 17, has been taking care of the two younger children after school and helping her mother with the housework and meal preparation. The family is on a marginal income, and the family agency would have to pay for either the nursing-home care or for the housekeeper. There would be little difference in cost. The function of the caseworker is to help Mrs. Allen evaluate the choices. Should she choose the services of a housekeeper, she would have the comforts and the pleasant atmosphere of her own home. It would be comforting to the children to have their mother at home, even though bedridden. The children have been somewhat threatened by Mrs. Allen's illness, and the youngest has expressed fears of being deserted by the mother. On the other hand, if she chose a nursing home, she might get better physical care, where a trained nurse would be in attendance. Recovery would probably be speeded because there would be less responsibility for Mrs. Allen. Moreover, the housekeeper would not live with the family, and Mrs. Allen needs some assistance during the night. Since both plans have advantages and disadvantages, and diagnostically they are both possible and workable, the role of the caseworker would be to help Mrs. Allen explore her feelings and to support her in whatever decision she finally made.

Miss Clark, an unwed mother, 20 years old, came to the attention of the agency after the birth of her child. She was faced with making a plan for herself and the baby. Her family, well known in the community, gave some thought to keeping the child; it could provide financial support, but it feared the community gossip. Her sister could adopt the child, but that would mean that the child would be raised in the same community. The child strongly resembles the mother, and there is fear that in time the people of the community would notice this resemblance. Miss Clark's third alternative is to release the child for adoption, but she has strong negative feelings about doing this. The function of the caseworker was to assist the client in examining the possible plans and in helping her to evaluate them realistically. Throughout this relationship the caseworker's sensitivity to the feelings of the mother were vital. She was stimulated to talk out her feelings and to clarify her own mind. It became quite obvious that the first two possibilities had too many difficulties, and that adoption was the most realistic choice. The client was able to work through her guilt feelings about adoption, and with the support of the caseworker decided upon that course of action.

LIMITATIONS TO SELF-DETERMINATION

The principle of client self-determination can become a meaningless cliché, however, if the client's right is not balanced realistically with the limitations to that right. A person's freedom to choose and decide is not synonymous with license. The rights of one individual are circumscribed by the rights of other individuals in society. The right of the individual is accompanied by the duty to respect the right of others. Human freedom is a means, not a goal in itself; it is a means for attaining the legitimate proximate and ultimate goals in life. It cannot, therefore, sanction self-injury or injury to others.

Specifically related to social casework, the client's right to self-determination has four limitations:

1. *The client's capacity for positive and constructive decision making.* No method or principle can be applied rigidly with universal sameness to every client and to every problem. Just as casework generally is individualized in accordance with the differentials in the client's personality, his need, the function of the agency, and the competence of the worker, so also the principle of client self-determination is individually applied. The ideal of each client's being fully self-determined must be modified by the realities in each individual instance. Since the capacity to make decisions varies from client to client, the worker is aware of the client's mental and physical capacity to act for himself and does not force him to self-determination beyond his capacity. The incapacity of the client, however, is not freely presumed by the worker. Rather, the assumption should be that the client is capable of making his own constructive plans and decisions. This assumption is sustained until the worker has clear evidence, or at least a prudent doubt, concerning the client's capacity for decision making. The capacity of the clients has degrees. The evaluation of this capacity is one of the more important skills in casework.

Some clients are able to keep the full responsibility for the direction of their own situations. Others are too weak to assume full responsibility and need the active support of the caseworker. Temporarily, the caseworker may have to share some of the responsibility in the case of some clients. This, however, is done only to the degree that the client is incapacitated.

Caseworkers have differed in their evaluation of the capacity of unmarried mothers, as a group, to make sound decisions.[9]

Some feel that the unmarried mothers are so damaged emotionally that they are incapable of arriving at a good decision themselves. These caseworkers have expressed the conviction that they must guide, "steer," and "take sides in" the final decision. Other caseworkers seem to have a higher evaluation of the ability of unmarried mothers for self-determination. Both agree, however, that each unmarried mother's ability should be individually evaluated. The function of the caseworker is to study the mother's social, cultural, economic, and psychological pattern, to help the mother work through her emotional problems, to acquaint her with the resources available to her, to help her consider realistically the factors in the possible choices and plans, and thus to help her make a decision about her child.

In casework with children, adolescents, the aged, and the mentally retarded the caseworker may have to be more or less active, depending upon the capacity of each client.[10] Plans may have to be made for the client. In some cases the caseworker may have to assume an authoritative or executive role in order to protect the client from the very probable results of his own confused planning. In such instances, however, the caseworker continues to seek the client's participation by interpreting what is being done and why.

A few clients may be so impaired in their ability for adjustment that they need to be treated as socially sick persons. In extreme instances, in emergencies, the caseworker may have to act as quickly "as an ambulance surgeon," especially in the case of "the very ill or ignorant or inarticulate"; but these instances may be rare and will be recognized by the caseworker who generally follows the principle of client self-determination.[11] Refusal to share the responsibility with such clients would be equivalent to a refusal of service.

Mrs. M had two children, 2 and 4 years old, in foster care for six months with a private agency. Now she wanted to remove the children from the foster home, where they were making an excellent adjustment, and take them to live with her in an apartment. Mrs. M was an alcoholic. In one of the episodes, about seven months ago, the father had taken the children and left the home. He had obtained a divorce and physical custody of the children, but was willing to allow Mrs. M to arrange for their care. Mrs. M was very upset. She was filled with guilt feelings because of her behavior, unhappy at being separated from her children; she wanted a reconciliation with her husband. She was physically and emotionally run down, and on regular occasions drank heavily. Diagnostically, it was quite clear that Mrs. M was not ready to assume the care of her children and that the children should remain in the foster home for a while longer. The role of the caseworker was to help Mrs. M accept foster care for the time being, while assisting the mother with her personal problems.

Mr. R was brought to a V.A. hospital following an alleged suicide attempt. At the time of admission he said that the suicide attempt followed rejection by a girl friend. He also told that, when he was in the Army, while driving with his fiancée, he had an accident in which she was killed and he suffered a fractured back. During the first interview the patient said he wanted to be a policeman and asked whether his hospitalization in a mental hospital would interfere with this. The caseworker said he did not know, but suggested that, in order to plan wisely, it might be good to discuss what work the client did in civilian and Army life, what he liked to do, why he wanted to be a policeman, and whether there were other things he might want to do. This was agreeable to him, but he kept returning to the topic of being a policeman. Before the next interview a review of the claims folder revealed that the accident had involved four servicemen returning from a furlough, that the patient had not been driving the car, and that no one else was injured in the accident. The Rorschach, T.A.T., and other psychological tests indicated no suicidal, homicidal, or schizophrenic tendencies, but a basically immature, dependent, and emotionally unstable personality. The psychiatrist thought it unwise and unrealistic to participate in any plan toward the patient's becoming a policeman, both because of the patient's own limitations and because of the hospital's responsibility toward society. The caseworker continued to see the client, and the topic of becoming a policeman continued to be discussed with a therapeutic goal rather than for actual social planning.

2. *Limitation arising from civil law.*[12] Authority and law are realities of organized society. During the last twenty years caseworkers have discussed the relationship of the concept of authority with client self-determination and generally have agreed upon the compatibility of the two. Caseworkers are primarily interested in the skills whereby the clients are helped to accept and adjust to the limitations of personal freedom arising from law and authority. The general purpose of law is to prevent the individual from abusing or misusing his liberty and to protect society from such abuse. The experience of caseworkers has been that normally clients are willing to accept and adjust to the limitations set down by legitimate authority. Some of the socially and mentally ill have a neurotic or psychotic aversion to any form of authority, and these need special care. Others have a hostility, not to authority itself, but rather to the authoritative *attitude* of those who administer it. An authoritative attitude is described as a rigid, emotional, domineering manner wherein the person of the administrator of the authority is made to appear as the only basis of the authority. Such an attitude in a social caseworker is destructive.

The authoritative approach, however, is sometimes necessary and useful in casework, but it must be delicately and skillfully used. The authoritative approach is described as the use of a legitimate, objectively existing civil law or ordinance. In those public agencies where the caseworker is actually or equivalently a public officer, the authoritative approach may be frequent. In private agencies and in public nonauthoritative agencies the authoritative approach may seldom be used, except as a last resource in circumstances of imminent serious danger to the client himself or to other people. The function of using coercive force to compel submission to authority is avoided by caseworkers and delegated to licensed public servants.

In using the authoritative approach the spirit, the manner, and the attitude of the caseworker are all-important. The use of authority is individualized and related to the capacity of the client and to the realities in each case. In agencies exercising a protective function, as in probation and parole, and in child-placing agencies there are certain areas in which the client's choices and decisions are defined by law; there remain, however, many areas in which the client is free to make his own decisions. In a public assistance agency the law determines the eligibility requirements which the applicant must meet in order to receive financial assistance. The client's freedom in this area is limited in the sense that he must give evidence that he is eligible. Beyond that limitation, the client has the right to determine for himself fully. The caseworker considers authority as an item in the client's reality situation, and by means of the casework skills and techniques helps the client to accept and adjust to the requirements established by law.

Mr. and Mrs. A separated. She had been given temporary custody of their child pending the divorce proceedings. At the time of the preliminary hearing Mrs. A testified that her husband had been abusive to her; she obtained an order restraining him from visiting the home and from seeing the child until the divorce hearing took place. Mr. A told the caseworker at the family agency that his wife's charges were untrue, that he had not been abusive, and that his wife was negligent in caring for the child. Despite the restraining injunction he planned to go to the home, abduct the child, and leave the state. In so doing he would make himself liable for contempt of court and for kidnaping, if he took the child out of the state. Mr. A stated that the child was his as well as his wife's, and that the court could not tell him what was best for his child's welfare, since he loved the child and would do what was best. Mr. A felt free to express his hostile feelings toward his wife and toward the authorities. In helping Mr. A to talk through his feelings and his problem, the caseworker was able to get him to the point where he was able to accept and adjust to the limitations of his personal freedom arising from law and to consider other plans of action. The caseworker acquainted Mr. A with community resources available for help with problems such as his. He was referred to Legal Aid, which assigned an attorney to plead his case in an effort to gain permanent custody of the child. He saw his problem more clearly and in so doing he was able to conclude that his initial plan was not a good one for himself or for his child.

Mrs. B, an ADC recipient with two young children, requested to be removed from the ADC rolls. She was deserted by her husband three years ago and has not heard from him since; the marriage has not been legally dissolved. She has never been able to accept the idea of public assistance. She was asked how she intended to support the children. She could go to work, she explained, but she did not want to leave the children during the day, nor does she want housekeeping service. She has extra rooms in her home which could be rented, but she objects to strangers in her home. Recently she received a proposal of marriage from a stable, dependable man. She told this man that her first husband died. In order to be removed from the ADC payroll, and because she really cares for this man, although she said that she did not feel she loved him, she is willing to commit bigamy and marry him. Throughout the weekly interviews, which lasted over a period of many months, the caseworker by means of a good relationship helped Mrs. B to express and clarify her feelings, to avoid entering into a bigamous union, and to remain on the ADC roll, a more realistic plan for herself and her children.

3. *Limitation arising from the moral law.* The natural right to make choices and decisions about one's own life does not extend to moral evil; a person might have the physical power to

make such a choice, but he has no real right to do so. Ordinarily, the choices confronting the client in most casework situations are within the framework of moral good, but cases do arise in which the client is inclined to a course of action which is immoral. A caseworker who operates within a well-integrated philosophy of social work does not assume an air of indifference in such a situation, but helps the client to avoid such a decision. The realistic worker knows that a morally out-of-bounds decision may be a source of future problems, perhaps worse than the one which is being avoided by illicit means. Such situations may raise perplexing problems, especially when the caseworker and the client subscribe to different standards and codes of morality. These problems need to be faced and resolved on the basis of principle rather than by an amoral expediency.

Many of the commonly accepted moral laws, such as those prohibiting stealing and murder, are covered by the civil law. In some cases, such as divorce, sterilization, and abortion, the civil law may legislate some restrictions while the Church contributes additional restrictions. Some moral laws are a part of the Church's legislation only.

The caseworker, especially when he is of a different religion than the client, must respect the conscience of the client and help the client make choices and decisions which are within the boundaries of that conscience. If the client violates the moral law and acts contrary to his conscience, he does spiritual harm to himself. This not only produces psychological difficulties for the client, such as guilt feelings, but it also does spiritual damage. The caseworker needs to have a real conviction about the ontological reality of spiritual values. The caseworker is not promoting the total welfare of the client if he helps the client to solve a social or emotional problem by means which are contrary to the client's philosophy of life.

The case of a client who is considering remarriage after a divorce from a valid marriage can serve as an illustration of this difficult area. There are three possible situations: (1) both the client and the caseworker are of the same religion, which prohibits such a marriage; (2) the remarriage is contrary to the client's religious beliefs but not to the caseworker's; and (3) it is contrary to the caseworker's religion but not to the client's. In each of these situations the caseworker needs to be clear about his role in regard to client self-determination.

In the first situation, in which remarriage is contrary to the religious beliefs of both, the role of the caseworker is to help the client avoid the immoral action by helping him to solve the problem in some other way. The caseworker helps the client to express his feelings, to clarify them, to develop insight into the full meaning of remaining within his own moral code, and to explore alternative plans. The caseworker refrains from any activity which would be equivalent to cooperation in the violation of the moral law. In most instances a referral to a clergyman may be indicated.

In the second situation, in which remarriage is contrary to the religious beliefs of the client but not of the worker, the caseworker helps the client remain within his code, because for the client his religious beliefs are a reality in his environment. An early referral to a clergyman may be imperative. To help the client remain true to himself in times of stress, when he is tempted to violate his own principles, is a great service to him. The longview welfare of the client is thus promoted. If the client eventually decides on the immoral course of action, the caseworker does not help in implementing the decision, for this would be a disservice rather than a service to the client.

In the third situation, in which remarriage is contrary to the religious beliefs of the caseworker but not of the client, a few basic principles of human conduct need to be considered. The principles are these: the client has a right to follow his conscience; the caseworker does not impose his own standards upon the client; the caseworker has a right to his own conscience and his own integrity, and therefore he has the right to refrain from co-operating in that which he believes to be wrong. In practice, therefore, the caseworker helps the client to discuss and clarify the decision. But if the client decides to remarry, the caseworker cannot cooperate in implementing the decision, because by so doing the caseworker would be cooperating in something which he considers wrong.

4. *Limitations arising from the agency function.* Each social agency, whether public or private, has been established to perform a more or less specifically defined function in the community. To achieve its purpose the agency has the right and the need to establish limitations to its services. These boundaries are incorporated into agency function and are concretely expressed in rules, standards, eligibility requirements, and kinds of services offered.

The client has a corresponding duty to respect this right of the agency. If he wishes to use its services, he is obliged to remain within the framework of the agency function. He has no right to services or assistance which are beyond the scope of the agency's function or for which he is not eligible. If his application for service is a voluntary one (that is, not required by law), he is free to terminate his contact with the agency that does not offer the service he desires and to seek that service elsewhere. Referral aid, of course, would be offered to him.

ENDNOTES FOR PRINCIPLE 6

1   Lucille Nickel Austin, "The Evolution of Our Social Case Work Concepts." *The Family* 20:43, April 1939.
2   Helen C. White, "Activity in the Case Work Relationship," *The Family* 14:208-14, October 1933; Hamilton, "Helping People—The Growth of a Profession," pp. 294-95.
3   Mary Hester, "Field Teaching in a Private Family Agency," *The Family* 22:14-20, March 1941; Harriett M. Bartlett, "Emotional Elements in Illness: Responsibilities of the Medical Social Worker," *The Family* 21:42, April 1940.
4   Eleanor Neustaedter, "The Rôle of the Case Worker in Treatment." *The Family* 13:151-56, July 1932.

5 Fern Lowry, "Objectives in Social Case Work." *The Family* 18:263-68, December 1937.

6 Robinson, *A Changing Psychology in Social Case Work*, pp. 115-50.

7 Bertha Capen Reynolds, "Between Client and Community." *Smith College Studies in Social Work* 5:98, September 1934.

8 Leah Feder, "Early Interviews as a Basis for Treatment Plans." *The Family* 17:236, November 1936.

9 Erma C. Blethen, "Case Work Service to a Florence Crittenton Home," *The Family* 23:250-51, November 1942; Ruth F. Brenner, "Case Work Service for Unmarried Mothers," *The Family* 22:211-19, November 1941; Sylvia Oshlag, "Surrendering a Child for Adoption," *The Family* 26:135-42, June 1945; Leontine R. Young, "The Unmarried Mother's Decision about Her Baby," *Journal of Social Casework* 28:27-31, January 1947; Frances H. Scherz, " 'Taking Sides' in the Unmarried Mother's Conflict," *Journal of Social Casework* 28:57-58, February 1947.

10 Donaldine Dudley, "Case Work Treatment of Cultural Factors in Adolescent Problems," *The Family* 20:249, December 1939; Lillian L. Otis, "Intake Interview in a Travelers Aid Society," *The Family* 22:50-51, April 1941; Martha E. Shackleford, "Case Work Services with Retarded Clients," *The Family* 23:313-14, December 1942; Joan M. Smith, "Psychological Understanding in Casework with the Aged," *Journal of Social Casework* 29:189-93, May 1948.

11 Gordon Hamilton, "Case Work Responsibility in the Unemployment Relief Agency." *The Family* 15:138, July 1934.

12 Crystal M. Potter and Lucille Nickel Austin, "The Use of the Authoritative Approach in Social Case Work," *The Family* 19:19-24, March 1938; Gordon Hamilton, "Basic Concepts in Social Case Work," *The Family* 18:150, July 1937; Lucille Nickel Austin, "Some Notes about Case Work in Probation Agencies," *The Family* 18:282-85, December 1937; David Dressler, "Case Work in Parole," *The Family* 22:3-6, March 1941; David Dressler, "Case Work in an Authoritarian Agency," *The Family* 22:276-81, December 1941; Stephen H. Clink and Millard Prichard, "Case Work in a Juvenile Court," *The Family* 25:305-07, December 1944.

Principle 7

CONFIDENTIALITY

SOCIAL WORK touches human life more intimately in many ways than many of the other helping and healing professions. The caseworker, either in a home visit or in an office interview, is frequently the observer and regularly the recipient of confidential information concerning the client and his family. It may be a fact, a series of facts, or a situation in the client's life which he shares with the caseworker or allows the caseworker to observe, with the implicit or explicit understanding that the caseworker preserve the information as a sacred trust.

Confidentiality in social casework can be considered from two points of view: as an item in the professional code of ethics and as an element of the casework relationship. The latter, based upon the former, will receive the principal emphasis in this chapter.

The principle of confidentiality appears to be deceptively simple at first glance, but actually is very complex and difficult to apply to concrete casework situations. It is based on philosophical principles which are generally unfamiliar to caseworkers, and it poses puzzling questions to which the profession up to this time has devoted comparatively little thought. It can be defined in the following terms:

> **Confidentiality is the preservation of secret information concerning the client which is disclosed in the professional relationship. Confidentiality is based upon a basic right of the client; it is an ethical obligation of the caseworker and is necessary for effective casework service. The client's right, however, is not absolute. Moreover, the client's secret is often shared with other professional persons within the agency and in other agencies; the obligation then binds all equally.**

When the client applies for help or service at a social agency, he realizes in some way the necessity of revealing pertinent facts about himself and his situation to the caseworker. This may include, in some cases, his innermost feelings, which he wants no one else to know about. It may include facts about previous behavior which, if generally known to his friends or neighbors, would detract from or destroy his personal reputation. It may include "skeletons in the family closet" which are a source of embarrassment to him.

He communicates this secret information upon the condition, at least implicitly made, that it is necessary for the help he is seeking. He assumes that the information will not go beyond the persons engaged in helping him. He definitely does not want to exchange his reputation for the casework help he is seeking.

He enters the casework relationship with that understanding. Therefore the caseworker's preservation of secret information is an essential quality of the relationship. If a client ever became aware of an individual caseworker's violation of confidentiality, the relationship would be destroyed.

THE RIGHT TO CONFIDENTIALITY

The natural law is the foundation of all human rights and duties, of every real code of ethics, including the principle of confidentiality in social work. Any code of ethics which is not based on the natural law is no more than a list of social amenities.

The natural law is the will of the Creator as manifested in nature. Because of the infinite intelligence of the Creator each created thing is assigned a function and a purpose. As long as the thing performs its function, order reigns and there is a serenity and a growth in its life. The natural law, as it pertains to human living, is written in the heart of man by the loving God. Living according to that law is not only an obligation, but it is the source of man's peace, his growth, and his happiness. Concretely, the natural law spells out man's duties to himself, to his fellow men, to his family, to society, and to God.

The means for the fulfillment of these duties are called rights. The human person has two classes of basic natural rights. The first is the right to life; the second is the right to growth and development. Each of these is actually a cluster of rights.

The right to growth and development includes (1) the right to procure the good of the body; the right to the basic necessities of food, clothing, and shelter for the conservation of life and the proper physical care of the body; (2) the right to the good of fortune, which is the right to acquire private property; and (3) the right to the good of the soul; the right to the emotional, social, intellectual, and spiritual development of his personality. This is precisely the basis of the client's right to confidentiality in social casework. These rights are necessary means for the performance of duties prescribed by the natural law, through which man strives toward his happiness, his destiny in life.

Every person, therefore, has a natural right to his secrets. The thoughts of a person's mind and the affections of his will are subject only to the scrutiny of God, except those that the person willingly communicates to other persons. The right to secrecy usually is not an end in itself but a necessary means to protect other rights.

As with material things, the person has the right to the possession, the lawful use, and the disposal of his secrets. Since a person has dominion over his secrets, he may use or dispose of them in any lawful manner. If he reveals them to another person, he may impose his own limitations on the confidant in the use of the secret information.

An invasion of a person's secret contrary to the owner's will, even if no other damage to the owner results, is a theft. A revelation of a secret, even of one which was lawfully obtained, which is revealed in a manner contrary to the conditions imposed is a violation of justice.

The person's right to secrecy, however, is not absolute. As will be discussed later, this right as every human right is limited by law, by the rights of other persons, and by the rightful good of society as a whole.

ETHICAL OBLIGATION OF THE SOCIAL WORKER

Confidential information can be defined as a fact or a condition, or the knowledge thereof, pertaining to a person's private life which is normally hidden from the eyes of others. There are three classes of confidential information: the natural secret, the promised secret, and the entrusted secret.

The natural secret is information which, if revealed, would defame, injure, or unjustly sadden the person. The obligation to preserve natural secrets binds everyone, regardless of the nature of the relationship. It may have become known by a relative, a friend, a stranger, or a professional person. It may have become known to a social worker in an unofficial manner, outside the professional relationship. Usually it is information which would injure the reputation, real or apparent, of the client. To reveal to others the true but hidden delinquency of a person is an ethical violation known as detraction. The basis of the right to natural secrets is man's natural right to his reputation. The social worker, therefore, has the obligation to safeguard such information concerning the client even when the information became known to the social worker as a private individual, provided of course that another person's right does not supersede the client's right.

The promised secret is one in which the confidant gives an assurance, a promise, after he has learned the secret information, that he will not divulge it. The subject matter of the promised secret may include the defamatory facts of a natural secret or it may include nondefamatory facts about the client's personal life which he does not want revealed.

The entrusted secret is information which is communicated to a confidant with the previous explicit or implicit understanding that the matter will not be revealed. The subject matter may or may not include a natural secret. The entrusted secret implies a contractual agreement between two persons which binds the confidant to secrecy even when the matter is not of a defamatory nature.

In social work confidentiality includes all three types of secrets. Most commonly, however, the professional secret in social work is an entrusted secret. Even if the client does not explicitly verbalize the contractual nature of the revelation, and even if the client does not say "I will give you this information only on the condition that you do not reveal it," the presumption always is that an implicit contract is made. Therefore the caseworker has an ethical obligation, arising from the implicit contract, to keep the confidence. Social workers have had no need to theorize about the nature of the ethical obligation, because their consciousness of being professional persons always inclined them to accept confidentiality wholeheartedly.

This obligation is stated in the professional code of ethics for social workers in the following words:

> Respect and safeguard the right of persons served to privacy in their contacts with the agency, and to confidential and responsible use of the information they give.[1]

CONFIDENTIALITY IN SOCIAL WORK
A GROUP SECRET

When the client reveals secret information to the caseworker there is or should be an implicit understanding that the matter is being communicated not merely to the individual caseworker but also to the social agency. The justification for the group secret is twofold: (1) the caseworker is not a free-lance welfare counselor but an agent of a social agency; (2) the agency cannot give effective service unless the information is shared with other persons within the agency.

When the client confides secret information to the caseworker, therefore, it can be validly presumed that the client understands that the information will be recorded in the case file, that it will become known to the typist, to the supervisor, and to anyone else who is participating with the caseworker in serving the client through ordinary procedures of the agency.

Social work is not alone in extending professional confidentiality to a group or a team. In the medical profession, for instance, the physician, the recipient of the original confidence, must share information with nurses, technicians, attendants, orderlies, and clerical workers, insofar as they need to know it in the line of serving the patient.

Even though the confidential information is extended to many persons, the obligation to confidentiality is not lessened. It binds equally every person who shares in it.

In most instances the presumption of the client's understanding of the group secret, at least in a vague and lay manner, is clear and simple. In a few cases, where the content of the secret is rather unusual, it may be desirable or necessary to discuss explicitly with the client the nature of the group secret. If the client objects to the recording of certain facts and the help of the agency can be given without the information, then the facts should not be recorded. If the client objects to the recording and the information is needed for the functioning of the agency, then the caseworker would need to interpret this to the client, with the view of helping the client decide whether he still desires the services of the agency.

The biggest difficulty concerning the ethical use of the group secret is the establishment of a policy concerning intra-agency and extra-agency divulgence of secret information. The obligation to define the policy rests with the administrator.

In intra-agency sharing of secret information the agency needs a clear policy which determines the persons who genuinely need to share in the secret information and the extent to which they need the information.

> There must be *objectively*, and not merely in fancy, some line beyond which those necessary disclosures will not pass. If no such line can be drawn, if there is no real limit to the area in which the divulgences are made, the bottom falls out of the whole relationship as far as its confidentiality is concerned; and the situation becomes at one and the same time a wholesale betrayal of confidences and forfeiting of professional dignity.

> In the assumption that the client's consent to partial divulgences can be reasonably presumed, the confidential treatment consists in well-ordered communication of the secret to those persons and only to those persons who can be licitly included in the presumed consent. It includes, first of all, the recording of the confidences in the case record. This process of recording entails a partial divulgence within the Agency, for the record is typed by members of the clerical staff. The supervisors and other official members of the Agency have access to the recorded con-

fidences and the worker discusses the confidences at regular intervals with the supervisor. The staff meetings frequently discuss the recorded material so that the other members of the staff come to know the details of families being served by other workers. These divulgences are all made within the official family of the Agency and are consistent with the principles of entrusted secrecy in the presumption that the presumed consent of the client is at the base.[2]

In extra-agency sharing of secret information—that is, sharing such information with other social agencies—the consent of the client should normally be secured. When that is not possible the valid presumption that the client would give his consent if he were asked is necessary. The presumption is not valid if the revelation to others would cause harm to the client's welfare of soul, mind, or body. Each agency has the obligation to define its policy in this matter and to draw a clear line beyond which it does not share information with groups outside of the agency. For the formulation of a truly workable policy the participation of the staff is highly desirable. This can insure detailed ethical procedures to cover most situations.

Where should the line be drawn? The answer to the question is not easy. . . . The whole relationship, in its extended formality, is based on the presumed consent of the client. How far does that presumed consent allow the social work set-up to go in making partial divulgences? Positively, that consent can be reasonably presumed to permit divulgences all along the line where it is clear that the divulgence is demanded for providing the type of service which the client wants and which he would be unreasonable in not permitting the social worker to provide even though it means the divulgence to other Agencies. Negatively, that consent cannot be presumed when the divulgences, even within social Agencies, would lead to serious embarrassment or serious physical inconvenience of the client. . . . In a general sweep it draws the line this side of all law enforcement bodies and all public departments where the knowledge of the client's confidential information might lead to extreme embarrassment, loss of material goods, or loss of personal liberty.[3]

THE CLIENT'S RIGHT
TO CONFIDENTIALITY LIMITED

No human right is absolute. Every right is limited either by a higher duty of the individual or by the rights of other persons. Specifically, the client's right to confidentiality is limited by (1) a higher duty to himself, (2) the rights of other individuals, (3) the rights of the social worker, (4) the rights of the social agency, and (5) the rights of the community.

Since the natural law is the source of all rights and duties, there can be no real conflict between the client's right to confidentiality and the limiting duties and rights. The problem, then, which in some cases may be a very perplexing one, is to determine whether another right or duty is greater than the right to confidentiality, or whether confidentiality supersedes them. In an actual case, however, the apparent conflict may be so extremely difficult to resolve that a consultation with persons specially qualified to assist in a solution would be necessary.

In the following brief discussion of the five classes of possible conflicts in the practice of social work only the general principles involved will be indicated.

1. *Conflict within the client himself.* An apparent conflict may exist between the client's right to preserve his secret and another of his rights or duties. The solution of the conflict requires a weighing of the rights involved. Care must be taken not to exaggerate either side. The presumption, however, should always be that the right to confidentiality remains dominant until clear evidence to the contrary appears.

2. *Conflict with the rights of another individual.* In some cases the client is so vitally connected with another person that preservation of the secret would constitute a serious harm or damage

to the other person. In other words, the preservation of the client's secret may appear to violate unjustly the rights of an innocent person. Here again an examination and a weighing of both rights is necessary. And the right of the client should prevail until there is clear evidence that the preservation would constitute a grave damage to the other person.

3. *Conflict with the rights of the social worker.* When the client communicates a secret to the social worker, the latter becomes aware of an obligation to keep the secret inviolate. In some rare instances the social worker may realize that keeping the secret would involve the forfeiting of his own personal rights, rights which seem to have a greater importance than the right of the client. The social worker cannot be expected to surrender his own personal natural rights in the performance of his professional duty. As in the previous two situations, the conflicting rights need to be examined, weighed, and resolved. If it becomes clear that the caseworker's rights are dominant, he may licitly reveal the entrusted secret if it is necessary to avert a grave damage to himself. The reason for the licitness is the presumption that the caseworker could not conceivably have bound himself to secrecy in that manner at such prohibitive cost to himself.

4. *Conflict with the rights of the social agency.* Every agency, whether public or private, has been organized with a definite purpose; thereby it has assumed some very specific duties toward individuals, families, and the community generally. These duties are specified in agencies by the kinds of services offered and the conditions under which they are offered. Corresponding to these duties are specific rights, which are the necessary means for fulfilling the duties. A situation may arise in which, by keeping the secret of the client, a right of the agency would be endangered or violated; in keeping the client's secret, the agency would be forced to act or not to act contrary to its purpose, contrary to its rights and duties. The principle in the solution of this conflict is the same as in the situation above, namely, the principle

of the preponderant right. The agency would not be bound to preserve the secret of the client if thereby the agency suffered a serious harm. Such situations happily are extremely rare, but when they occur they can create considerable consternation in the staff of the agency.

5. *Conflict with the rights of society as a whole.* This is a conflict between the individual good and the public good, between the individual right and the common welfare. Society has the duty of promoting the public good, of maintaining peace and good order, and of building programs which positively promote the physical, intellectual, and moral welfare of the members of the community. The individual person, on the other hand, since he is a social being, has the obligation as a citizen to cooperate with his fellow citizens in maintaining and promoting the common good, even when it means the limitation of some of his apparent rights. Some of his basic rights, however, are inalienable, which the common good cannot insist on his surrendering. Other rights, nevertheless, must be surrendered when it is clear that their use would jeopardize the common good. The solution of such conflicts, as in all the other classifications of conflict, is the relative weight of conflicting rights. The general principle is that the obligation of the entrusted secret ceases when the preservation of the secret would constitute a real and a serious damage to the common good.

When a caseworker is confronted with any of these situations, which hopefully are not too frequent, the manner of the caseworker in the interviews is of great importance. As the conflict of rights is being clarified, possibly with the aid of a professional ethician, and as the solution takes shape, the caseworker must remain a caseworker through the process. Even though the solution happens to be a hard one for the client, making imperative the revelation of the client's secret, the caseworker is expected to strive to maintain a good casework relationship with all of its desirable qualities. This includes the same sensitivity and response to feelings as in other cases, the nonjudgmental attitude, acceptance, and, in short, the fullness of humanity which is expected of a professional social worker in dealing with people in need of help.

AGENCY POLICY CONCERNING CONFIDENTIALITY

Because of the intricacies of the ethics of confidentiality, the agency has a responsibility of spelling out in policy fashion the practical application of the principles for the caseworkers. A particular agency, offering defined services and located in a specific community with definite resources, can and should identify those questions and issues concerning confidentiality which commonly arise in that agency. Once identified, they can be resolved in the light of the general principles; thus a well-defined agency policy can be formulated and thereby the abstractness of confidentiality becomes concretized.

The best statement of general principles in the current literature of social work is found in a pamphlet written by the Washington, D.C., chapter of the American Association of Social Workers. This is its summary of principles:

Clients have a right to protection of personal information about themselves in their relationship with a social agency during and following the process of obtaining service, a right which may be superseded in exceptional situations. Recognition of this right requires adherence to the following principles:

I. The client should be used as the primary source of information about himself and information sought from him should be limited to that which is essential to provide service.

II. Within the agency information regarding a client should be revealed only to those persons and to the extent necessary to provide service.

III. Other agencies and individuals should be consulted only with the client's consent and within the limits of that consent.

IV. Only that information should be recorded and those records maintained that are essential to provide service and the use of records should be determined by agency function and the consent of the client.[4]

These principles, which at first glance may seem so simple and obvious, pose many difficult questions which individual agencies need to answer for themselves. For example: Is the information routinely secured from all clients really essential to provide service for each client? Does the increased understanding of human dignity and of the client's rights indicate a change in the use of the social-service exchange, other agencies, and collateral sources? May an agency freely use information in its own files about former clients when a relative asks for service? Under what circumstances is information released to the police or other law-enforcement agencies? Is it ethical to secure a blanket consent of the client to consult other agencies? Is it licit for a husband or a wife to give consent for the other in consulting other agencies? When can consent be validly presumed?

Legitimate differences of opinion on these questions may exist among agencies. The profession as a whole needs to take a clear stand on many of the issues raised by confidentiality; but in the meantime each agency needs to take its own stand, honestly and clearly. Otherwise the individual caseworkers will flounder in their practice.

CONFIDENTIALITY NECESSARY FOR EFFECTIVE CASEWORK SERVICE

Obviously, and happily, not every client has a secret which, if revealed, would make a dramatic headline in the newspapers. The confidences in day-to-day casework practice generally would be considered quite prosaic to the world at large, with exceptions at rare intervals. In most cases only the client's relatives, friends, or neighbors would consider his secret really "interesting."

Whatever the nature of the confidences, however, they are sacred to the client. And the client will not fully engage in the process of study, diagnosis, and treatment unless he feels that the caseworker likewise considers them sacred. He needs an atmosphere of confidentiality in the interviews rather than verbal reassurances, although these can also be effective. This atmosphere gives him a security to bring into the open the real, but very painful, facts of his environment and of his personality, and to do something constructive about them.

This trust in the caseworker is developed gradually as the result of a lot of little things. The lack of information concerning the agency on the return address of mail sent to the client, the absence of similar information on the agency's car in home visits, the care which the caseworker takes to avoid mentioning the client's name aloud in the waiting room, the instinctive lowering of the voice when there is a possibility of being overheard by others—these are some of the little things which go into the creation of the atmosphere. The most important thing, however, is the internal attitude of the caseworker which raises the ordinary courtesy in person-to-person relationships to a professional level.

ENDNOTES FOR PRINCIPLE 7

1 "Code of Ethics"; in *Standards for the Professional Practice of Social Work*, p. 5. New York: American Association of Social Workers, 1951.
2 Walter McGuinn, S.J., *The Professional Secret in Social Work*, unpublished dissertation, Fordham University; quoted in Robert E. Regan, O.S.A., *Professional Secrecy in the Light of Moral Principles*, pp. 200-01. Washington: Augustinian Press, 1943.
3 *Ibid.*, pp. 201-02.
4 *Principles of Confidentiality in Social Work*, p. ii. Washington: American Association of Social Workers, 1946.

SUMMARY

SOCIAL CASEWORK is a way of helping people who have psycho-social problems. It includes the processes of study, diagnosis, and treatment. These processes take place in an interview.

To help the client effectively the caseworker needs adequate knowledge of human behavior and of community resources. The caseworker needs skill to mobilize the inner capacities of the client and the appropriate external resources. Above all, he needs skill in the professional interpersonal relationship, which is defined as the dynamic interaction of attitudes and emotions between himself and the client.

The relationship is the soul of casework. It is a spirit which vivifies the interviews and the processes of study, diagnosis, and treatment, making them a constructive, warmly human experience. It makes casework a practical living out of a true democracy's philosophy of the dignity and worth of the individual person. It makes casework a truly professional service because it attunes the caseworker to the whole person and to the totality of the client's needs.

The client comes to a social agency with one or more expressed needs; they are sometimes called "the presenting problem." The client verbally expresses in varying degrees of adequacy his need or problem at intake. These expressed needs, however, are only a fraction of his needs.

All human beings have certain common basic needs: physical, emotional, intellectual, social, and spiritual. In adverse circumstances these common needs are felt with a special poignancy. The hypothesis in this study is that the following emotional and social needs, common to all people, become intensified when a person seeks help from a social agency: the need to be treated as an individual, to communicate his feelings, to be accepted, not to be judged, to make one's own decisions, and to have one's secrets kept confidential. Consciously or unconsciously, the client senses a danger to these basic rights and needs. The intensified awareness of these is the origin of the dynamic interaction of attitudes and feelings between the client and the caseworker.

This interaction has three directions. The first is from the client to the caseworker. The client, because he must reveal his problem and some of his weaknesses to the caseworker, has a fear that he may be treated as "a case" rather than as an individual, that he may be judged and condemned, that he may be forced to do something he does not want to do, or that his confidences may be revealed.

The second direction is from the caseworker to the client. The caseworker, principally through his over-all attitude which has some emotional content, assuages the fears of the client by communicating a respect for the client's basic human rights and for his integrity as a person.

In the third direction, again from the client to the caseworker, the client becomes aware of the caseworker's attitude and, in some manner, manifests this awareness to the caseworker.

These three directions are like forces moving in circle fashion; their beginnings and ends are imperceptible; actually, they are separable only conceptually. They are living, vibrant forces that endure in some degree throughout the life of the case.

Each of the seven principles of the relationship, discussed separately in the preceding chapters, is founded upon one of the intensified basic needs and includes the three directions of the dynamic interaction. *Individualization* is the recognition and understanding of each client's right and need to be treated as an individual who has unique qualities arising from his heredity, environment, and life's experiences. *Purposeful expression of feelings* is the recognition of the client's need for communication at a time when his problem is partially or predominantly emotional. *Controlled emotional involvement* is the recognition of the client's need to receive an appropriate response to his feelings. *Acceptance* means perceiving and dealing with the client as he really is rather than as the caseworker might wish him to be, maintaining all the while a sense of the client's innate dignity and personal worth. *The nonjudgmental attitude* is the recognition that the caseworker's role is to understand and help the client rather than judge or condemn him. *Client self-determination* is the recognition of the client's right and need to make his own decisions. *Confidentiality* is the preservation of secret information concerning the client which is disclosed in the casework interview. Each principle implies all the others; they are separable in concept only.

The casework relationship reveals the exalted professional ideals that beckon a social worker. He is expected to be both a firm-footed realist and a clear-eyed idealist. As a realist the caseworker is expected to see, understand, and help with the hard, sometimes ugly and repulsive, realities in the lives of his clients. As an idealist the caseworker is expected to recognize in a practical way the dignity and nobility of people who, in some instances, may have lost respect for themselves.

As an idealist the caseworker is the champion of the rights of individuals; as a realist he is aware that individual rights are limited by the rights of other individuals and by the common good of society.

As a realist he understands the importance of the emotional component in the lives of people who are in trouble; as an idealist he knows that emotional needs and problems, important as they may be, are not the most important considerations in human living. Without imposing his own standards and values upon clients, he tries to help them remain within objective social, legal, and moral boundaries.

As an idealist he sees each client as a precious child of the heavenly Father. As a realist he sees the client as he really is, with attitudes and behavior which perhaps are quite unlike to God's. With the motive of love, he strives for skill in the use of the wisdom of sciences to help his brother in need. The caseworker hopes that he is, in some small way, an instrument of Divine Providence.

IMPRIMI POTEST: William J. Schmidt, S.J., *Provincial of the Chicago Province,* January 7, 1957. NIHIL OBSTAT: Austin G. Schmidt, S.J., *Censor Deputatus,* March 7, 1957. IMPRIMATUR: ✠ Samuel Cardinal Stritch, *Archbishop of Chicago,* March 12, 1957.